T0318147

MARLENA GRAVES

SUZANNE STABILE, SERIES EDITOR

FORTY DAYS ON
BEING A NINE

ENNEAGRAM DAILY REFLECTIONS

An imprint of InterVarsity Press
Downers Grove, Illinois

InterVarsity Press
P.O. Box 1400, Downers Grove, IL 60515-1426
ivpress.com
email@ivpress.com

InterVarsity Press® is the book-publishing division of InterVarsity Christian Fellowship/USA®, a movement of students and faculty active on campus at hundreds of universities, colleges, and schools of nursing in the United States of America, and a member movement of the International Fellowship of Evangelical Students. For information about local and regional activities, visit intervarsity.org.

Enneagram figure by InterVarsity Press

Cover design and image composite: David Fassett

Interior design: Daniel van Loon

Images: gold foil background: © Katsumi Murouchi / Moment Collection / Getty Images
paper texture background: © Matthieu Tuffet / iStock / Getty Images Plus

ISBN 978-0-8308-4758-7 (print)
ISBN 978-0-8308-4759-4 (digital)

Printed in the United States of America ♾

InterVarsity Press is committed to ecological stewardship and to the conservation of natural resources in all our operations. This book was printed using sustainably sourced paper.

Library of Congress Cataloging-in-Publication Data
A catalog record for this book is available from the Library of Congress.

P   20   19   18   17   16   15   14   13   12   11   10   9   8   7   6   5   4   3

Y   37   36   35   34   33   32   31   30   29   28   27   26   25   24   23   22   21

For those who seek to move forward
by knowing the truth and
being set free to live.

WELCOME TO
ENNEAGRAM DAILY REFLECTIONS

Suzanne Stabile

The Enneagram is about nine ways of seeing. The reflections in this series are written from each of those nine ways of seeing. You have a rare opportunity, while reading and thinking about the experiences shared by each author, to expand your understanding of how they see themselves and how they experience others.

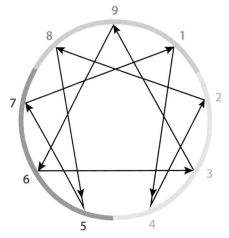

I've committed to teaching the Enneagram, in part, because I believe every person wants at least these two things: to belong, and to live a life that has meaning. And I'm sure that learning and working with the Enneagram has the potential to help all of us with both.

Belonging is complicated. We all want it, but few of us really understand it. The Enneagram identifies—with more accuracy than any other wisdom tool I know—why we can achieve belonging more easily with some people than with others. And it teaches us to find our place in situations and groups without having to displace someone else. (I'm actually convinced that it's the answer to world peace, but some have suggested that I could be exaggerating just a bit.)

If our lives are to have meaning beyond ourselves, we will have to develop the capacity to understand, value, and respect people who see the world differently than we do. We will have to learn to name our own gifts and identify our weaknesses, and the Enneagram reveals both at the same time.

The idea that we are all pretty much alike is shattered by the end of an introductory Enneagram workshop or after reading the last page of a good primer. But for those who are teachable and open to receiving Enneagram wisdom about each of the nine personality types, the shock is accompanied by a beautiful and unexpected gift: they find that they have more compassion for themselves and more grace for others and it's a guarantee.

The authors in this series, representing the nine Enneagram types, have used that compassion to move toward a greater understanding of themselves and others whose lives intersect with theirs in big and small ways. They write from experiences that reflect racial and cultural differences, and they have been influenced by different faith beliefs. In working with spiritual directors, therapists, and pastors they identified many of their own habits and fears, behaviors and motivations, gifts and challenges. And they courageously talked with those who are close to them about how they are seen and experienced in relationship.

As you begin reading, I think it will be helpful for you to be generous with yourself. Reflect on your own life—where you've been and where you're going. And I hope you will consider the difference between change and transformation. *Change* is when we take on something new. *Transformation* occurs when something old falls away, usually beyond our control. When we see a movie, read a book, or perhaps hear a sermon that we believe "changed our lives," it will seldom, if ever, become transformative. It's a good thing and we may have learned a valuable life lesson, but that's not transformation. Transformation occurs when you have an experience that changes the way you understand life and its mysteries.

When my dad died, I immediately looked for the leather journal I had given to him years before with the request that he fill it with stories and things he wanted me to know. He had only written on one page:

Anything I have achieved or accomplished
in my life is because of the gift of your mother
as my wife. You should get to know her.

I thought I knew her, but I followed his advice, and it was one of the most transformative experiences of my life.

From a place of vulnerability and generosity, each author in this series invites us to walk with them for forty days on their journeys toward transformation. I hope you will not limit your reading to only your number. Read about your spouse or a friend. Consider reading about the type you suspect represents your parents or your siblings. You might even want to read about someone you have little affection for but are willing to try to understand.

You can never change *how* you see, but you can change what you *do* with how you see.

ON BEING A NINE

Are you an Enneagram Nine or do you know one? I trust this book will be useful in helping you to better understand us. For you see, it's written by an Enneagram Nine. Me!

This book enfleshes a Nine's tendencies and dispositions. You will likely read along and find yourself saying, "Aha! Me too," and, "No wonder I do that!" It may very well lead you to bury your head in your hands and lament because you see in yourself that which you don't want to see—that which you wish for all the world did not exist within you as a Nine. It is true that learning about your Enneagram number will do that to you.

And yet, you will also be pleasantly surprised by joy, for you will see the loveliness others see, characteristics and gifts you always hoped were true of you. You'll see that others see this beauty, giftedness, grace, and power when they encounter you. You'll also look into eyes of delight and see yourself reflected back. And it is wonderful to be a Nine. We are indeed unique gifts to the world (as is each person reflected by each number). But Nines in particular need to know that, because in our unhealthy states we discount ourselves.

I first learned about the Enneagram in 2010 from my fellow contributors at *Christianity Today*'s Her.meneutics blog (content now available at christianitytoday.com /women). They talked about it in our private Facebook group, asking what our "numbers" were, and then went back and forth about it. I had no idea what they were talking about, so I did some initial research. (Indeed, I continue to research and learn much about the Enneagram and myself to this day.)

The Enneagram reminds me that weakness and sin lie within, yes, but there is also so much good in us—because we are made in the image of God. Not one of us are alike even though we may share in being an Enneagram Nine. Our personalities, experiences, physical makeups, histories, environments, ages, ethnicities, religious contexts, and many more factors make us unique human beings and unique Nines. What I'm getting at in these daily reflections is how my "Nineness" manifests itself. Hopefully, you will see more and more of how your Nineness manifests itself in your life, or the life of one you know. At the end of each reflection you will find a prayer, a reflection question or two, space to journal, or a spiritual practice to try out.

In this book, I am as honest as I can appropriately be about who I am. This is so because I truly believe that the truth sets us free from what shackles us to destruction, to that which is death-dealing. The truth sets us free to move forward in our life in Christ—to love God and our neighbors well. What I want you to know is that if you seek to move toward wholeness, holiness—toward life; that is, union with God—then you have to start by accepting the truth about who you are and then by telling the truth, especially as an Enneagram Nine. It can be good or not-so-good truth. But whatever it is, commit to doing it! I so strongly believe in the need for truth that I start out with it on day one. Fear not.

I am so glad you are coming along for this Nine ride. Certainly, if you find it helpful, tell others about it. And, one last thing: I would love to hear about your Nine adventures, either as a Nine or as someone in relationship to a Nine. May you flourish!

COMING TO TERMS WITH WHAT AFFECTS US

ONCE, TWO WOMEN IN my Christian workplace bullied me and continually sabotaged me. At first, I doubted it could be happening. I questioned my intuition and especially the evidence before my eyes because I couldn't figure out why they were attacking me.

When I started at the venue, they liked me. In fact, I was downright giddy because I thought I found two good friends after having moved to a new town. But, it was not to be. Soon enough, they started ignoring me. They blatantly refused to help me when I asked for help, even though they helped others and we were all supposed to help out each other. They put me down, made fun of me. They verbally and demonstrably communicated that they did not want to sit by me at meetings and at retreats. They rejected me and uninvited me.

I was told it was due to jealousy and envy over how my superiors treated me. They didn't like when my superiors praised me and gave me opportunities to use my God-given gifts. It didn't matter that I honestly praised them up and down and rejoiced in what they did well. It soon became a hostile work environment. I was harassed. The abuse factored into my leaving the position for something else.

The whole time, I tried to grin and bear it—to love my enemies: those who were slandering me, talking behind my back, and actively sabotaging my work. I didn't treat them like they treated me. It's what Jesus would do.

And truth be told, it was also a way of avoiding conflict. I was so upset by what they were doing to me I was scared I'd explode on them if allowed to let my pain and hurt leak out. I didn't say anything at first because I wasn't sure I could control my anger once I unleashed it. I sought to reconcile with the main aggressor to no avail. Finally, when I was pushed to the max, I told my superiors about the hostile work environment. It was extremely uncomfortable to be at odds with my Christian coworkers!

This kind of situation put my weakness, which is sloth— the vice of the Nine—on full display. Slothfulness could be actual physical laziness. And for some, it probably is. But one way we can think of it is that it's a failure to show up to life. One way we give into slothfulness is by avoiding disappointment and that which limits us. It is pretending to be unaffected, or wanting to be unaffected, or willing ourselves to be unaffected by not acknowledging the negative effects on us. Indeed, we might not even be aware of what it is we are feeling or are affected by. It is a self-forgetfulness of the unholy kind: avoiding ourselves. It is stubbornly refusing to come to terms with how we are being affected and limited. It's a penchant for avoiding conflict or hard things.

It's a proclivity to be asleep at the wheel of life instead of being awake. It is the proclivity to live halfheartedly, to give halfhearted attention to what is going on in us. Dealing with the messiness, the hard, and the sad takes too much energy. It is our unhealthy coping mechanism. As a result, we can have a hard time figuring out what we feel!

In that situation, I was trying to put on a brave face, to follow Jesus by loving my enemies but without admitting to myself, them, or others the profound harm they were doing to me because I was trying to keep peace in the workplace and in my soul.

And that's the thing about us Enneagram Nines. We have beautiful contributions to make to the world and we bring great value. But we will be healthier when we face ourselves and figure out, maybe with the help of trusted others, what we have been avoiding, escaping, and trying to be unaffected by. It's the path forward for us in Jesus' name.

We will not grow healthy and whole until we are willing to face ourselves. We face ourselves by acknowledging the truth and engaging life instead of avoiding it or white-knuckling life so as to be unaffected and keep the peace. Truth-telling and facing ourselves are the first steps toward wholeness and holiness.

Are you willing to face yourself and move forward in grace? What are you avoiding or suppressing so as to be unaffected? Maybe today you will take a step to acknowledge it. Confide in someone you find wise and trustworthy and who loves you.

THE INTERRELATEDNESS
OF ALL THINGS

ONE OF THE HIGHLY PRONOUNCED qualities in our lives is the profound knowledge—indeed, the lived conviction—that all things are interconnected. This is a truly beautiful feature of Nines and one of the many gifts we bring to the world. Who you and I are, how we live, our thoughts, our words, and our actions have lasting effects on everything and everyone around us. This is true whether we or anyone else are aware of it. God knows. And others who know us *are* aware of this facet of us. We have a way of weaving seemingly disparate fabrics together into a beautiful tapestry so that others might glimpse the reality of the big picture while also noticing the fine details. We are seers. Observers.

It is why when I am in my kitchen and would rather forego the slight inconvenience of cutting up the plastic-type netting that holds soft drinks together that I wonder to myself, *What if this doesn't get recycled, and fish or other marine life get trapped inside it?* So, I take the thirty seconds to snip, snip, snip the rings with a pair of scissors. I toss it into the recycling bin, hoping it will indeed be recycled and not wind up on a barge sailing from continent to continent and turned away from disposal. The same with clothes. I wonder, *Do I really need a pair of shoes or another outfit?* And if I do, I think, *Why not buy secondhand so my clothes don't end up in landfills?* Our action or inaction affects all living things. Our environment. People.

We could talk about our words. We damage our loved ones *and* those we hold in contempt. We are responsible for our words. Even if they remain unspoken in our hearts, they affect our posture toward others and ourselves.

But the littlest good in us affects all things in some mysterious way too. Doing our part to recycle and care for the environment and the animals is effectual, even if minutely so. Taking evil thoughts and slanderous words captive before they reach our mouths and are spewed into the atmosphere is effectual. Speaking life-giving words every chance we get to those with whom we interact makes all the difference in the world. Seemingly inane and little actions are the means of overcoming evil with good (Romans 12:21). How you and I take care of our bodies will not only affect us but also those around us because our bodies affect our emotions and spiritual perceptions and vice versa. Do you see how it's all related?

What we do or don't do, what we say or don't say forms our postures. We need the grace of God's Spirit and healthy, trustworthy community to overcome evil with good. Remembering that all things are connected will motivate us to live whole and holy lives with the help of God and the beloved community.

As we live "whole," our lives will affect generations to come. Threads of beauty and goodness can be traced to how we lived and loved—and whether future generations can trace it to us particularly or not, it is true.

God has made your life one of the icons of the goodness and interrelatedness of all things. This is true for every person, but Nines symbolize it in a particular way. Our ways of living draw seemingly disparate strands of life together and weave them into a beautiful tapestry. Our lives are windows toward heaven, scenic views where much can be seen. Yes, we certainly have our weaknesses—details that need to be worked out in God's way, in God's time, with our cooperation. But showing others how all things are related is something to celebrate and for which to give thanks.

Do you see the interrelatedness and connectedness of all things? In what ways might you offer that as a gift to others?

OUT WITH IT!

"WHY DO YOU HOLD BACK?" a mentor asked. "You have so much more to offer!" she exclaimed. The same question and comment have been echoed by others close to me in some form throughout different periods of my life. I was surprised they had picked up on my holding back. The simple reason is, I fear running over people with whatever power, intellect, skills, and abilities I have. I know what it's like to be run over and rendered invisible. I don't want to do the same to others. The problem is, I held back for so long that I inadvertently rendered myself invisible.

That is the trap Nines can find ourselves in. Unlike others who have to practice keeping their mouths shut, we have to practice speaking up. We have to be very intentional about it, or we'll regress.

Maybe there are reasons we fail to speak our opinions. Maybe we don't have an opinion; we simply don't know what we think. Or perhaps we can see both sides of an issue; seeing both sides most often has something positive to offer. We fear coming down on one side will displease, offend, or alienate others. And that runs counter to our natural disposition of gathering people together in unity. We want everyone to get along, to see the good in others, despite our differences. We get along with diverse cross sections of individuals from across the political, religious, class, and ethnic spectrum, even if we're not on the same page about everything. Why can't others?

So, out with it. Let's offer our opinions and stances if we have them. I know it's uncomfortable and hard, but we have contributions to make to the world! We have God's gifts to steward. When we fail to speak up, we are doing ourselves and the world a disservice. Don't worry; I am not advocating that we vocalize everything that crosses our minds. That's foolishness. But I am saying we need to speak up much more than we have historically been comfortable doing.

It's okay to say "I don't know" on controversial issues where we haven't made up our minds yet. It's okay to be on the journey whether or not one side or the other complains, even loudly, at your current inability to stake your claim. That is spiritual and intellectual honesty. But it's dishonest to not speak up for fear of rocking the boat or displeasing another.

Do you make your desires known?

Where is one area in your life where you need to speak up?

Practice speaking up this month and sit with the discomfort and see what happens.

THE GIFT OF SILENCE

GROWING UP, THE TELEVISION WAS ALWAYS ON. Constant noise in the background. For the most part, I couldn't stand it, although every blue moon I would watch *Knight Rider* or *The A-Team* or *The Fresh Prince of Bel-Air*.

For my soul, a droning TV was like scraping nails on a chalkboard. My mom liked (and still likes) the television on whether or not she and Abuelita or anyone else in my family were watching it. I suppose it kept her company in the loneliness and isolation, given that my mom went from living in Manhattan and Puerto Rico to living in rural Northwest Pennsylvania. And, on the rare occasion that the TV was turned off, the radio was on.

Then again, maybe it wasn't the TV per se, but the soap operas and daytime talk-o-drama shows that got under my skin. I had no problem listening to radio preachers at night, as early as ten years old, when anxiety over familial issues kept me from sleep.

When I couldn't take the TV or familial conflict anymore, which was frequent, I'd escape into the fields or woods surrounding my home. Sometimes I'd hide under a bush, peering out at the world, disguised. I wanted to be alone. I wanted peace. I could only find it outside in God's creation, which is still my go-to.

I've been married almost twenty years, and we've never had cable. We had a TV for a short time so my husband could watch football or so that I could watch documentaries late at night on PBS when I was pregnant. Then we kept a TV so we could play DVDs of cartoons we rented from the public library for our oldest daughter. But we haven't had a TV in years. No Hulu. No Netflix. I *did* gift YouTube TV to my husband so he could watch sports on our computer. Otherwise there is no television for me.

Even before we had children my husband used to joke that we lived in "Hermit's Cave." I was the monastic, contemplative hermit who loved silence. Coming home to silence after having been at work or school all day was and is a gift. Although, we now have three young daughters who most definitely do not have my silent, monastic bents. The only time I have a modicum of silence during their waking hours is when I'm in the bathtub, and even then it's interrupted every ten or so minutes. But what sweet bliss is to be found in those intervals of silence.

As Nines, we seek peace. In an unhealthy place, we seek peace at any cost. But in a healthy state, peace rejuvenates us and energizes us to go back out into the world to love and serve our neighbors. Silence and accompanying solitude afford us the opportunity to recollect ourselves. To dream, to plan, to breathe. I have dubbed them "recreating silences." Being alone with God in the silence of my room, or on my seat by the window, or on our front porch with the sounds of cars whizzing and bees buzzing all bode well for me. So do personal favorites of mine: the silence that burrows into my bones and into my soul deep in a forest; a stream gurgling its sounds with me in its midst; the hush of the ocean on a barely populated beach.

Of course, such silence and reverie become destructive if overindulged to the point we are neglecting others and our responsibilities. But for us, it is a necessity if we are to hear God, to be whole, to love others well, and to be who we are meant to be in the world. Silence is God's gift to us and allows us to share our gifts with others.

Do you practice silence or do you run away from it? Why?

Notice when retreating into silence and solitude is rejuvenating and when you are using it as a form of escape.

AVOIDING CONFLICT?

WHAT THEY SAY ABOUT US NINES is that we are conflict-avoidant. Yet for me in particular, I wouldn't say that's true most of the time (but of course as I mentioned on Day One, I do have it in me). If the poor and marginalized are being attacked, if the underdog is being picked on, you better believe I am going to say something in writing or in person. Maybe that's the principled part of the One wing. So I am not afraid to speak up. And I'm not afraid to speak up with my ideas at meetings or give my opinion. Perhaps this is a level of health. Who knows?

I do know I don't like hurting people's feelings. And maybe that's where conflict avoidance comes into my life. Perhaps I should put it this way: in the past, I preferred not to hurt people's feelings. So I didn't express my anger or protest unless pushed to the limit. As a result, I did all sorts of gymnastics to avoid hurting others' feelings. However, that led to my own harm. And again, I don't like to be hurt and therefore don't want to hurt others. Add to that the command to love our neighbor as ourselves, the admonitions not to slander one another, not to say or do what we wouldn't want to be said or done to us. Now you see our dilemmas as Nines. I have one caveat here: I'm talking about people outside my immediate family—I'm more direct with them.

As a teenager I got into all sorts of messes because I didn't want to hurt people's feelings, especially guys. It nearly ruined me. But somewhere along the way, I learned that avoiding conflict by avoiding what I took to be hurting people's feelings didn't result in peace.

Now, granted, I've been told by those who don't know my insides well that I have the patience of Job. It's not true. I think it's more that I have a slow fuse. Or maybe as a Nine I repress my feelings for a long time. But I know and my family knows that if I do that and am under stress, then that fuse will eventually ignite an explosion like Mount Vesuvius—and that doesn't work.

Nines can and need to be assertive when necessary. It doesn't mean we're doormats. Jesus himself did not evade conflict. How many times does he say, "You have heard it said . . . but I tell you . . ."? Didn't he call Herod a fox? That resulted in conflict!

I think about Jesus' conversation with the woman at the well (John 4:4-26). Though he spoke to her lovingly, he didn't avoid potential conflict with her. And she didn't avoid potential conflict with him. Honestly, I am struck by how frank she was with Jesus. She was a truth-teller. Assertive. A thinker. The Eastern Church even knows her as a saint: St. Photini. She could've given Jesus water and ran. But she engaged him, and he her—both rather assertively—and look what health resulted for her through their interaction.

Telling truth and living truthfully put us on a pathway to salvation where God can engage us, and we can engage God. Only when we tell the truth can we move forward into healing and *shalom* and become who we are meant to be in God, and therefore, for the world.

How are you avoiding conflict?

Practice engaging in conflict, not inciting it—unless necessary. You know what I mean: protecting the poor, vulnerable, and powerless, even if that person is you. For example, what truth are you not telling that needs to be told, because you fear hurting another's feelings?

EXERCISE

I DON'T LOVE TO EXERCISE, at least at the gym. I think it is because now that we have children, we have to be able to get all the girls going and their things together so that we can head out. Or, I always wonder now if I should instead spend the time doing, folding, and putting away laundry. I work full-time, have three girls, all with their activities and schedules, plus Shawn's work schedule and activities, plus whatever we do outside of work and school and activities as a family. It's a constant juggling.

So maybe I should say I don't like exercising while trying to juggle everything—including the unforeseen, like my own sickness, the girls' sicknesses, or whatever schedule changes come our way.

After Shawn and I were first married, we used to get home from work, crash for a bit, and then leave to go work out. We used to work out together two hours a day, four days a week. Faithfully. For years. (In college, friends thought of me as a runner. I laughed at that because I never thought of myself as a runner. Never. I ran for mental health and because I figured it was the easiest way to keep healthy. But at twenty-three years old, a sports doctor told me to cease and desist from running because of my knee problems.) Now we still work out, but it's a lot harder. Going to the Y is a family affair. What I do like is playing tennis with Shawn alone, but we are unable to do that at this point. I don't count walking in metro parks as exercise, though I suppose it could be. I have no problem doing that as often as I can. It's one of my favorite things. Though it's harder in the snow and ice in the winter, and I have less motivation to do so on such days.

Why give the details of my family life and my struggles with exercise? Because I believe that for me to exercise is an act of love not only for my body and for myself, but my family, God, and others. It is easy to be in my head, to think about things, to be in my spirit, to pray. Such disciplines of disengagement are not my issue though they are issues for others. But by engaging my body, I demonstrate that I am someone who believes that our bodies are important. My body is not meaningless or a trap. Christian tradition deems theology, thinking, and behavior that flows from denigrating the body as false teaching. Therefore, I will take care about what I do with my body, what I eat, and what I drink.

I didn't mention the limitations of my body except for the knee problems. I have asthma that can creep up as well as other aches and pains. Another limitation I have is the need for surgery but not the money for the surgery. And despite all the good it does me, again and again, especially after a flu or cold, I have to recommit to exercising. Because I've realized that for me failure to exercise, when I still have the ability to exercise, is a lack of love.

Engaging the body (and emotions) is different for each person. It could be something like having a good cry. It could mean dancing or going on a walk. And for some who are depressed, getting out of bed and getting dressed is the greatest miracle. And for that, we thank God. When we get in motion with our bodies, whatever that looks like for us—hear me, I am not talking about exercise per se, but whatever is motion for us—that will allow us to keep in motion. Think about how you might need to engage your body and emotions. How will you do it?

WHO AM I?

"*LOOKING FOR A REASON, / Roaming through the night to find, / My place in this world. . . .*" In sixth grade, these lyrics to the song "Place in This World" by Michael W. Smith resonated deeply with me. By twelve years old, I already felt lost. Not sure where I belonged. I didn't feel home at home or in school. I suppose I felt the most at home at church and outside in creation. And when I was reading my Bible.

In college, I had trouble figuring out my major. I only knew I wanted to help people. My dad and high school guidance counselor wanted me to be a medical doctor. So I started out as a pre-med major my freshman year, but I couldn't stand chemistry and biology. I was not interested in looking at slides. My grades were fine but lower than ever from lack of interest and from chronic stress worrying about whether I could even afford to stay the first semester.

Then I wondered if I should be a nurse so I could travel overseas and help the poorest of the poor. But the thought of bodily fluids grossed me out, though I hear some nurses say you get used to it. I then majored in psychology because I decided I would be a marriage counselor.

I was struggling mightily about my place, especially because I had to move off campus second semester of my freshman year. I lived with a generous elderly woman who allowed me to stay for free in her apartment but who was awkward and almost nontalkative—even smiling seemed difficult for her. So we were both hurting in different stations in life. More than twenty years later, my guess is that she was probably an introvert, tired of talking all day, and didn't have any more to give when she arrived home. I felt guilty for struggling with her personality, especially since I generally get along with most people. I also think she remained depressed over her decades-ago divorce.

I too fell into a depression over having to be off campus and from the great isolation from my peers. They couldn't come over, and I didn't have money to eat in the school cafeteria very often. I also had unforgiveness toward myself because of mistakes I made in high school as well as anger and unforgiveness toward my parents. I never had the opportunity to be a child because I had to parent my parents and siblings. That was on top of the strained relationship with my generous benefactor.

My junior year I moved back onto campus as an RA. That helped a lot. But in the midst of my agony over what to do with my life and what major to choose, one of my professors offered a compliment in an effort to be helpful but which didn't serve much use: "Marlena, the problem is, you're good at a lot of things. That's why it's so hard for you." Eventually I landed on a history major. I minored in philosophy and Bible (which was required at the school I attended), and secondary education was my emphasis.

Who am I? Where is my place in this world? What is my purpose? It can be incredibly difficult to figure these things out as an Enneagram Nine. In particular, I know it has been for me because it seems I have a piece of all the numbers. I thought it was over in college, but it wasn't. I switched jobs several times as we moved for my husband and graduate school. Oh how I would have loved to be one of those people who knew I would be a lawyer, teacher, scientist, carpenter, stay-at-home parent, bus driver—whatever— since early childhood. But I'm not. Why this desire to nail it down through a career as if a career says everything about who I am? Maybe it's the stability I craved.

Even now I can't pick one thing. But I do know this. At any given moment, I reveal what is at my core: I am a teacher, pastor-theologian, advocate, and writer in no particular order. A poet and creative with a bit of flourish.

Name some defining things that are true about you. What do you like? What do you dislike? Have you found a place in this world? If not, I invite you to begin the journey home.

SLICK, FANCY, NICE! PLAIN? WHAT?

READING THROUGH DESCRIPTIONS of the Enneagram, I am often annoyed by the description of how Nines dress. The idea is that we are plain and unassuming. When I hear that, I think, *Dour. Boring. Uninteresting.* I never like the description of the Nine's clothing style. It doesn't fit me at all. Perhaps it fits others, and the words I take offense at are words that they interpret as *Sensible. Down To Earth. Not Showy.*

I can be downright slick sometimes—colorful, artistic. "An urban hippie," as I once was called by friends who determined that urban hippie was my style. I actually agree. Maybe that means I am moving to my Enneagram Three health: enjoying being the star of the show.

Pish posh. Perhaps it's the Puerto Rican in me. Or could it be a combination of everything? Who knows? My point is that the Enneagram is a helpful tool for our general dispositions. For our strengths, weaknesses, and ways of being in the world. It's a helpful general guide, but can never tell the whole story.

We are far more than our Enneagram number and wings. We are a mystery made in the image of God. Our ancestors' histories, where we were born, our boundary places, our environments, and a whole host of other factors go into making us who we are. So we use the Enneagram as a most helpful guide, realizing that it is not the gospel truth. That it doesn't encapsulate who we are. There's no reason to stress if we still have questions.

Who can tell the measure and beauty and depth of a life? God can. And in that we can be at peace.

What parts of the Enneagram don't you understand or agree with?

I invite you to converse with another Enneagram Nine familiar with the Enneagram to see if you have similar questions. While the Enneagram captures much, it doesn't capture everything about us.

SEASONS OF OUR LIVES

WE NINES LIKE OUR COMFORT AND ROUTINES. When they are disturbed by life events or by others, we can come undone. We get depressed. Or resigned to it, we numb ourselves. We grow bitter. Or in anger we fight against it, fuming and thrashing about.

If anything is true it's this: life is anything but ideal. If, perchance, we find ourselves experiencing an idyllic state, we can be sure it won't last very long. It never does. Someone or something will burst our bubble. Disturb the peace.

Life is hard in a thousand different ways and also good. We can expect the good, hard, and mundane at the same time. I think about how when we are young, we have energy but often not the wisdom or experience to harvest it. When we are older, many of us have wisdom and experience but lack youthful energy and exuberance to fully live out our dreams and ideals. Life doesn't cooperate with our agendas. So what do we do when we have the wisdom and not the same amount of energy or freedom from responsibility?

Think of life in terms of seasons. Ecclesiastes 3:1 tells us, "There is a time for everything, and a season for every activity under the heavens." Some cringe when they hear the term "seasons of life." But their cringing has no bearing on the truth of the matter, does it?

In my twenties, my husband and I were graduate students, youth leaders, and I worked for a nonprofit. We'd go all day and part of the night and then collapse into bed. Now, we are older and have three daughters for whom we gladly care. They have their school schedules and after-school and weekend activities. And Shawn and I, two introverts who function as extroverts, have less energy and time. We cannot do what we want to do when we want to do it—even now that we have more income! Such is life. We wouldn't trade our daughters for the world. Nevertheless, we cannot be involved in all the ministries and activities we'd like to be involved in. It's the stage of life we're in: parents to elementary-aged girls, and one nearly a teenager.

Perhaps your age and energy level now hinder you from doing what you want to—you aren't going to be able to try out for the Olympics. Something is limiting you. It could be mental health. Or physical health. Or lack of finances. In this season, think about how you can live well to the best of your ability. How can you serve God and others within your limits instead of giving up or giving into resignation? He knows what we can and can't do. There's no need to beat ourselves up over what we cannot do and be. He only asks that we offer up our life as it is. If all we can offer is a widow's mite, then so be it. God accepts our smallest offerings as holy.

What are the gifts and limits of this season?

ENDLESS DEBATE, PARALYSIS

AS A NINE, IT CAN BE extremely hard to make a decision because we see the many sides of an issue, and we can become paralyzed. Some years ago, I was invited on a retreat with a group of folks I admired. What a gift! While we were retreating at the Franciscan Center in the foothills of the Rocky Mountains in Colorado Springs, we had the opportunity to sign up for a time of prayer and discernment. I signed up for a time slot because I was at a crossroads and was agonizing over which way to go. For years I had been waiting on God for an open door but nothing at all seemed to be happening. My angst was coming to a head. I was hoping that in prayer with spiritual leaders of depth, I might receive guidance from the Lord.

When it was my turn to be prayed for, I left our large group gathering. I crossed the veranda to where the trusted intercessors were waiting for me in a small conference room. I had a full half hour with them. To begin with, they asked me to talk about the struggle I was facing. I explained my situation, they asked me a few questions, and I glanced over to see the clock ticking—my time, nearly up. After listening to me, they conveyed some incredible affirmations. And then they began to pray, expressing what they sensed they heard from God. Suddenly one said, "Marlena, maybe all of this time you've been waiting on God, but God has been waiting for you."

What a bombshell! God waiting on me? Me? For nearly a decade I have been waiting on God! The retreat was in June. All summer I pondered, treasured these words in my heart, the way the Virgin Mary treasured Gabriel's message to her (Luke 2:19).

Summer quickly turned to fall. In September, I was listening to a sermon by an Eastern Orthodox priest on Ancient Faith Radio. He was referring to the Scriptures, but I cannot now recall anything about the sermon. All I heard was what jumped out through the radio and straight into my soul: "Pick up your mat and walk" (John 5:8). That was Jesus' command to the paralytic. But it became the word of the Lord to me. *Stop debating and take the next step, Marlena.*

"Take up your mat and walk." Jesus scandalized me with his command. "Who, me? Jesus, are you calling me a paralytic?" I continued, "If I do anything it is engage! I mean, after all, while it's not a word I use for myself, people do call me an *activist*!"

After having had time to reflect, I realize that after hemming and hawing for so long, because I didn't want to move forward until I knew clearly which direction to move in, the Lord had to metaphorically shout to get my attention. He had to nudge me by hinting that I was the paralytic in the story. I scoffed at the thought. But once again, telling the truth in this situation means confessing to years of paralysis. I was so scared of going the wrong way that I didn't move.

For Nines there is a point where indecision moves from being wise and careful to toxic. After all, it has been well and repeatedly said: "No decision is a decision."

Is God waiting for you? What is one step you can take? Consider talking to mentors and friends who know you well and can function as a committee of clarity to help you along.

IDEALIZING OTHERS

WE CAN'T HELP IT THAT WE initially see the ideal in a person, putting them on a pedestal. This is true with people we admire. We get all starry-eyed; we're idealists. It's the Nine way. But how do we cope when others fall from our pedestal of grace?

I remember I absolutely loved an ultra-famous musical group. I knew the words to every one of their songs on their two albums. I could point out all the nuances and intricacies of each song. Oh, the beauty and character of the lead singer's voice! The depth of the lyrics! The musicianship! Shawn knew of my love for this group and grew to share my admiration. So one day he surprised me by taking me to see them in concert. After the concert, I asked Shawn if we could stick around so we could meet them. It turned out to be a bad idea.

Women were fawning over them, hanging around right outside of their tour bus. When Shawn and I approached them, they ignored us. Me. Made me wonder if they would've paid attention to me if I were alone or with a female friend. I felt slighted. Not only that, but all the admiration I had for them went out the window. How could such a beautiful person and band, with such beautiful lyrics, with such deep soul, straight-up ignore me, ignore us? Didn't they know what avid fans we were, how much deep admiration I had for them? I don't easily give my admiration away. Well, when it was all said and done, I couldn't find it in my heart to listen to them much anymore. I still don't. What a pity!

Another time, I met an author that I admired and found him to be too cool toward me and others. His disposition didn't jive with the warm and magnanimous personality I imagined him to have when reading his books. I was severely disappointed. Afterwards, I conveyed my feelings to Shawn. And then Shawn pleaded with me, "Do me a favor. Do yourself a favor. Quit meeting writers and other artists you admire. You'll be disappointed, and we don't need any more of that." I have pretty much taken his advice.

All of this may sound foolish. Maybe the group I mentioned was exhausted. And truly, maybe they weren't interested in women they had no chance of inviting onto their tour bus for a fling. Maybe they had depth but also a penchant for promiscuity. Maybe the author I admired is an introvert. Most writers are. Who knows? He could've been having a "horrible, no good, very bad day."

I have got to cut these folks some slack and realize that for whatever reason, people aren't always putting their best selves forward. Human beings are complicated. I am complicated. Catch me in my weakness and disintegration, and you might not like me much. All of us, even the best of us, are a mixed bag.

So that's why Paul told the Ephesians to be "humble and gentle," to bear "with one another in love" (Ephesians 4:2). I need to think more about how people love me in all my complicatedness, in my distortions, in letdowns. Shawn loves me in all this. He bears with me knowing full well who I am, and I do the same. The least I could do is offer gentle grace to the great disappointers in my life—the grace God and others offer me. Seeing myself for who I am allows me to bear with others in love.

Are you idealizing someone now?

How do you cope with disappointment when those you've idealized fail to meet your expectations?

PROVISION

I GREW UP POOR—THE KIND OF POOR where I'd come home on many occasions to an empty refrigerator. I received free lunches in school. I can recall times when my parents couldn't afford to fill our home's fuel tank in the winter. That meant no heat until another paycheck or until we cut enough wood to sell to others, or to use for ourselves in a fireplace that didn't quite work: it often filled the whole house with smoke. And so I smelled like smoke from the burnt firewood when I climbed onto the school bus in the morning and throughout the school day. Kids remarked about it and made me feel more self-conscious than I already was. The smoke permeated the house; the warmth only partially filled our living room. The bedroom upstairs that I shared with Abuelita was an icebox. So, on days when we didn't have any heat, I slept with a jacket and covers piled on top of me. Crawling out of bed was akin to jumping into an icy river.

For my husband and I, following Jesus means we don't have lucrative jobs. I don't mean that the Lord is against high-paying jobs. What I do mean is that fulfilling our calling means that we aren't going to be bringing in the big bucks. While our jobs have been meaningful and fulfilling, we can think of plenty of other options to choose from if making money and living the high life were our primary goals. Of course, I know we are far richer than almost everyone in the world given we live in the United States. I tell you all this as background.

Recently, I was laid off due to budget cuts at the nonprofit where I worked. I didn't see it coming, and my husband and I have no safety net. Our families aren't able to help us out too much either. Plus, we had just spent our emergency fund on—wait for it—an emergency. I was in shock, teetering on despair because trusting God for finances continually requires much of me. And yet a great cloud of witnesses sprang into action to get us through a few months. Hallelujah! It is in this context that the words of the Gospel of John came to life in me as I prayed. "Where shall we buy bread for these people to eat?" Jesus asked (John 6:5). And then John tells us: "He asked this only to test him, for he already had in mind what he was going to do" (John 6:6). Jesus was asking Philip how they were going to feed a five-thousand-plus crowd (given there were women and children present too).

I find myself asking how we are going to acquire our daily bread. I am an Enneagram Nine whose second strongest instinct is self-preservation. (More on that later.)

I am inclined to think about such things when I am wondering how we will make ends meet.

Shawn's income doesn't cover our monthly expenses, which include our mortgage and car payments. Will I find a job that covers our needs and in which I can be somewhat present to my family? I have a lot of questions and few answers right now. And yet I am struck that when Jesus queried Philip about what could be done to feed thousands of people, the apostle John interjects this background information into the account: "He asked this only to test him, for he already had in mind what he was going to do" (John 6:6). God already has in mind what God is going to do for us even if I, like Philip, have no idea. I believe this, though in this moment, I cannot tell you how it is going to work out. God will provide creatively, and probably not in a way I can foresee. I have long stopped trying to figure that out.

In what area(s) is your trust weak? Is there an impossible situation in which you don't see a way forward?

Can you believe that God is taking care of you in this situation?

God is a good Father looking at us with love and delight. We are his beloved children. Let us sit with this remembrance: goodness and mercy will chase us down all the days of our lives as we dwell in his house, in him (Psalm 23:6).

Don't downplay or stuff your feelings. Tell God and others how you feel.

EXERTING OURSELVES AND TRUSTING GOD

THE VIRTUE OF AN ENNEAGRAM NINE IS ACTION. We are wonderful "actors," when we do act. Getting to the point of actions is the key. When we think about becoming healthy, our thought should be to exert ourselves.

Some personalities, some people, they don't know how to rest, how to sabbath. We are experts in sabbathing, in contemplation, in getting in touch with what matters in life. The key for us is not to stay in our heads. Not to be content to be in the mind alone while shirking active duty in life. We are not the ones who have to work hard at humility and kindness. Those are our natural bents. No my friends! We need to harness our energy in concert with God and the beloved community's energy. We have to get into the boat of our lives and set sail. Indeed, let us even be the captain, or rather, co-captains with God!

John 6:16-21 tells the story of Jesus' disciples in the boat. First of all, they had to actually get into the boat. After they rowed for some time, the wind began to howl. The waves grew bigger and bigger. In the middle of all this stress—the dark, waves getting higher and higher, the fear they felt for their lives, them wondering where Jesus was—they saw a figure approaching the boat. It was Jesus, making his way over to them as he walked on the water. Did he walk through the rough waves or did they suddenly become placid as he placed his foot on each part? We don't know. But as Jesus approached, he told them not to be afraid. When they heard his voice, they relaxed and welcomed him into the boat. John 6:21 tells us that after they were willing to let him climb into the boat, "immediately the boat reached the shore where they were heading."

When we exert ourselves, when we obey God, taking the steps that God wants us to take, and welcome God into our boats—that is, into our lives—we will reach the shore, where he intends for us to arrive. As Nines, we are not going to reach where God would have us go if we hold back. We will not move forward unless we exert ourselves. Remember, our virtue is action. Our vice, our tendency, is inactivity.

Have you allowed God into the boat of your life?

Think of one area in your life where you need to take action but instead have been indolent or inactive. What action step can you take to move in the direction that God would have you move?

PUTTING PEOPLE AT EASE

DESPERATE, WORN, AND DOUBTING, he hobbled into our conversation weak and vulnerable. He reached out to Shawn and me, telling us, "I trust you both." At the beginning of the conversation we sat with bated breath, bracing ourselves for what we were about to hear. We had no idea what he was about to tell us.

He proceeded to recount how for years he had the opportunity to witness the life of his pastor up close and as a result was left wounded. This pastor's lack of health and wholeness inflicted pain on those around him. It wasn't a case of sexual indiscretion or assault but of greed and power, of "ruling over," and of ruling with an iron fist. The pastor was self-absorbed and presented one face to the public and another to parishioners close to him. There is a phrase for that: "two-faced."

This innocent man is now walking around wounded and unsure about what type of association, if any, he wants to have with the church.

How do such folk as this pastor become leaders in the first place? Well, of course they are charismatic and gifted in certain areas. Obviously, they get things done by "hook or by crook" and legitimately as well. Maybe they bring in money or can cite a litany of public accomplishments. And people who ride on their coattails put up with it, because they or the organization somehow benefit despite what insiders experience up close. Fear of retaliation is legitimate; so they don't speak up because the price of speaking up is too costly. And so the damage continues. Speaking up might not change the situation. There is a real chance they and their families will be crushed.

I could do little but listen and hold space with this man who'd approached us. When he asked Shawn and me for input, we offered it, but only when he asked. I was honored he asked to share his story with us. At the end of the conversation he told us again that he felt comfortable and at ease and that he trusted us. Enneagram Nines do put people at ease and have an innate ability to understand where people are coming from. I'm the one who most often initially puts people at ease, while Shawn, who sometimes appears as a tall and imposing figure, and who is an Enneagram Five, most often asks just the right question to help bring clarity to a situation. We both understand that we can't fix things for people, but our presence, gifts, and posture remind people they are not alone and that there is a way forward.

Do you find people confiding in you? Have you found
that you are able to put people at ease by your very
presence? Contrast that with those who do not put
people at ease.

How can you use this gift presently?

GROWTH WITHIN BOUNDARIES AND LIMITS

WE NINES HAVE TO ACCEPT THE REALITY of our lives and not try to repress or deny it. That can be difficult. In each stage of life there are boundaries. Strictures. The sooner we accept that it is the case for all people, including us, the more quickly we can grow into health.

I can no longer live the life of my twenties. Back then, Shawn was in graduate school and I was in seminary. We were also working as codirectors of our church's youth group. Our days were full from dawn until dusk. Actually, past dusk—sometimes until 11 p.m. or midnight. Some nights I was so tired that I'd fall into bed exhausted without changing my clothes or brushing my teeth or removing makeup. I don't recommend it. But we had no children at the time and so had more time and flexibility in our schedules, although not very much income. Still, it was a wonderful time.

My thirties were wonderful and horrible and a blur. Wonderful in that I had our first daughter when I was twenty-nine and then our second and third in my mid-thirties. But I was basically on bed rest, sick, and incapacitated for all my pregnancies and for nearly a year afterward. After our second daughter was born, my ob-gyn said, "Your body is allergic to pregnancy—don't have any more children." And my thirties were wonderful in that I was a resident director on the same college campus where Shawn worked. Indeed, my thirties were rewarding in that I entered into the public stage of writing, where I published many articles for high-profile publications and got my first book contract. And yet my thirties were horrible because our campus was taken over by legalists—fundamentalists—who made life miserable for everyone. After we left those positions on the college campus, I had our third daughter. But parenting small children while working and writing, along with financial and work upheavals, left me exhausted. Neither Shawn nor I could live as we did in our twenties. We had more responsibilities, our bodies were changing, and we had three beautiful daughters to care for.

And now I am in my early forties. When I make decisions, I have to take my family into account. They are my closest neighbors that I am to love as I love myself. I can't always do what I want to do when I want to do it and how I want to do it without them being affected. Though our temptation as Nines is often to forget ourselves, our sin can also be to neglect others while off following our own pursuits.

Our lives are intimately connected. My family experiences the consequences of my action or inaction, for sloth is ultimately a lack of love. My spiritual, emotional, and physical health or lack of health affects them in one way or another even if I try to curb the ill effects of it. My time is not my own.

Obviously one need not be married or have a family to have limitations and boundaries in life. Boundaries and limitations come in many forms: age; financial considerations; physical, emotional, mental, contextual, geographical, social contingencies; and health. (Note, I am not talking about abusive situations. In that case, I pray you seek help.) Each one of us has boundaries and limitations. The question is, can God work and bless us within those limitations?

Well, I find that God works within our particular boundary lines and limitations, whatever they may be. Scripture tells us God made the nations from one person and marked out their appointed times in history and the boundaries of their lands (Acts 17:26-27). God seeks us and finds us where we are. God has appointed our times in history—where and when we were born, where we live, and our gifts. God is with us, right where we are. Right here.

Are you trying to transgress the boundaries and limits of your life? What are they?

How does transgressing boundaries affect you and others?

LEAD US NOT INTO TEMPTATION

I SAT IN THE PEW LISTENING TO soon-to-be Anglican priest Jason Lyon of Christ Anglican Church while on a trip to visit friends in Southern California. That Sunday morning, he spoke about the virtue of remaining steadfast in faith amid temptation.

In times of stress—especially as an Enneagram Nine—we simply desire comfort and relaxation: a reprieve, an escape from our pain and pressures. So, our way of handling stress and temptation might be to reach for the bottle or a prescription drug. Maybe we turn to pornography. Or social media. We might stuff ourselves with food to dull the pain. Or starve ourselves. It might be that we overwork, using busyness and productivity as a way to escape ourselves and our pain. Maybe we are in a state of denial about reality.

Using the serpent as a metaphor for temptation, Lyon observed, "A serpent challenges your intimacy with God. Temptation rarely has to do with the object presented to us, but with underlying desires." That is, it's not the alcohol, food, drugs, relationships, money, comparison, or anything else that ultimately trip us up. It is our desires driving our relationships to these things—desires such as greed, lust, or a need to be in control. When we don't get what we want, we might give God an ultimatum. In the words of Lyon, "If you're not going to do it, God, I am going to do it instead." That is, I'll find my own way of handling it.

For an Enneagram Nine, this means sometimes we'll move toward a Six in disintegration and stress. We become worried and anxious and seek to control our environments and others to get what we want.

We want relief, but when God doesn't come through on our schedule, when God doesn't act in a way we deem necessary and acceptable, we are tempted to go our own way to get what we want. That's true whether we are seeking relief from stress and pain or we're pursuing our own answer to unanswered prayer. We doubt that God is for us and instead believe God is against us. Otherwise, why isn't God giving us what we want?

Are there areas where we are taking our lives into our own hands? Here I am not talking about having goals and moving forward with the gifts God has given us. I am talking about trying to kick down doors or break open windows. Especially with Nines, I am talking about using illicit substances, pursuing illicit relationships, giving in to unhealthy habits—pursuing our desires in illicit ways, to numb the pain or to cope. When we do this, our relationship with God is challenged, as are our health and relationships with others.

Let us examine ourselves to see if we are in the faith, or if we are going the way of the tempter.

> Consider your unhealthy ways of coping with pain, stress, and conflict, which all come as part of being human. Knowing that, can you think of a healthy way to cope, flee temptations, and move in a healthy direction?

SCARCITY AND ABUNDANCE

"I AM CONVINCED THAT MOST OF our sin is a result of our feelings of scarcity," Nanny said.

Nanny is my friend Debby. But I've called her Nanny for over a decade, ever since she told our oldest daughter, Iliana, to call her Nanny. She and her husband, Carl, are nurturing parental-type friends—twenty years older than us—who are founts of wisdom and pastoral care.

Enneagram Nines fear loss. And so, I was fascinated when Nanny linked scarcity and sin, especially since she and Carl had recently lost everything: employment, community, houses, a car, and nearness to family. In the midst of such tremendous grief and loss, their beloved dog, Maggie, passed away too.

"Tell me more about what you mean," I implored.

She elaborated: "I believe we have a God of abundance, but we don't think so *because we think of abundance in terms of stuff and comfort*. But even in that, we have plenty of stuff in this country. It is mismanaged, hoarded, and not distributed appropriately. But our lack isn't because we don't have enough."

"What would you tell someone who has lost everything?" I asked.

"You can't necessarily say this to someone. They have to experience it themselves." Nanny meant that telling someone "God is enough," when they've lost everything, isn't wise or pastoral. "We had a safety net; we were able to live with our children, so we weren't on the street."

"What is abundance if not related to stuff and comfort?" I asked.

"Abundance has to do with our deepest desires. God is not stingy. God is love. And God's love is the most important thing, I think." Her voice trailed off. Amid all of the loss and grief, Nanny told me that she asked herself about her deepest desires. Yes, she wanted her own space, a house, a home. A dog. A community. For Carl to have a job. But what she really wanted, she confessed, was to be held and loved by God, to have a deep relationship with him. And that, she said, was "abundantly available" whether or not she possessed anything else. Abundance for the Christian, then, is having God as our treasure and love. God offers himself abundantly to us. This was the word from someone who had a series of unrelenting Job-like experiences.

"It doesn't mean that all this loss is not painful," she added. "I hope I don't lose everything again. But even after we lost everything, I found the presence and love of God to be abundantly enough."

As I listened, I witnessed a peace and strength, a shalom-filled matter-of-factness as she spoke.

"If I could only have one thing," Nanny concluded, "it'd be unity with God, to abide in God, as Jesus talks about in John 17:20-26."

What wisdom.

Do you have a mentality of scarcity or abundance? Be on the lookout for the abundance God has already provided for right now. You may have to pause and reflect. Consider this: a relationship with God is abundance.

FAITHFUL IN THE LITTLE THINGS

BEING FAITHFUL IN THE LITTLE THINGS, the quotidian of the everyday, is truly a miracle for Nines. It means we are living healthy. For example, I'd rather be writing or reading or socializing or teaching than folding or putting laundry away. Writing, reading, socializing, and teaching are so much more interesting to me. But folding and putting away laundry is a way to love my family. Though truth be told, I would love for more of them to participate in that act of love so that I don't bear the load alone.

Maybe for you it's not laundry. Maybe it's relationships. I know of Nines fastidious about laundry and household chores who neglect family and friends. Lack of effort to engage family members and friends has ill effects on those relationships. Nines can be guilty of neglecting the little things, which turn out to be quite big. Neglect is a way of showing a lack of love to those around us.

Maybe being faithful in the little, everyday things for you means exercising, intentionally keeping in touch with family members or friends, or something like taking out the trash. Whatever it is, it's the little things that matter and drive most of us crazy. Can we show some love to God and others by being intentionally faithful in the little things?

What does being faithful in the little things look like for you? Choose to be intentional about one little thing. Go about it quietly and see over time how it speaks love to those closest to you.

BURYING YOUR
TALENTS?

RESIGNATION. IT IS EASY FOR US NINES to resign ourselves to the forces and demands around us and to let the current carry us where it may instead of swimming upstream. It is our way of remaining in our comfort zones and avoiding conflict. Indeed, it is our modus operandi when our desire for comfort and self-preservation are out of whack.

About half a decade or more ago, I was tempted to give up writing. I was never that kid who wrote on reams of paper, knowing since second grade that I wanted to be a writer. I have friends like that. No, growing up I was just trying to survive the ill effects of poverty and other familial chaos. Much of my free time was spent with my dad and siblings doing chores and cutting wood so we had food to eat, and so my dad had money for gas to get to work. I was tired and burdened by life at a young age.

In college, I majored in history and minored in secondary education, philosophy, and Bible. I wrote lots and lots of papers. In seminary, my goal was to make my writing assignments—my papers—as beautiful and as interesting as possible. I wanted them to be works of art. It worked! My professors lauded my work, writing, and abilities. What joy!

In seminary, I also had a live radio show born out of a seminary internship. I had great freedom. The Christian radio station permitted me to choose my own playlist whether older or new songs, or songs in a different genre from the radio station's regular playlist. I took full advantage of that permission and also taught for ten to twelve minutes during the hour-long show that eventually went to three hours. Listeners regularly called in telling us that my words were convicting and asked for a physical copy of my messages. When we moved because Shawn landed a tenure-track position as a philosophy professor, I had to give up my show. I was devastated. And yet, that loss propelled me to start blogging and start writing my first book. Writing put me into a constellation of editors and other writers who emboldened me to take the risk of sending my first submission to a well-known Christian magazine. The rest, as they say, is history.

However, after ongoing suffering was coupled with seeing that the market and social media were flooded with writers—some good, some not—I wondered: *What's the point?* Why continue writing when so many are out there saying or hinting at similar things? It felt pointless. I felt invisible and as if my voice and work didn't matter—which is easy for an Enneagram Nine to feel. I communicated these feelings to God. And then, I sensed the Lord very tenderly and pointedly telling me, "Do not bury your talents. To stop writing is to bury your talents." God communicated nothing about the number of readers I would have nor how successful my writing career would be. God simply made it clear that to quit writing would be an act of unfaithfulness to both God and to my calling. So here I am.

Others, the devil and his demons, our own insecurities and lethargy, and our own measures of success will challenge our call to faithfulness. Do not bury your talents because you feel unappreciated and unsuccessful. As so many have said, Jesus was not successful by the world's standards. Progress in the kingdom of God— success—is very different from success in the world. We have to repeat this truth to ourselves and to others and then live by it. "Therefore, my dear brothers and sisters, stand firm. Let nothing move you. Always give yourselves fully to the work of the Lord, because you know that your labor in the Lord is not in vain" (1 Corinthians 15:58). Today when you feel discouraged, repeat to yourself, "Progress in the kingdom of God is different from progress in this world."

PARALYZED BY ANXIETY?

IN JULY 2015, I READ KATHRYN SCHULZ'S *New Yorker* article, "The Really Big One: An earthquake will destroy a sizeable portion of the coastal Northwest. The question is when." The article sent shockwaves throughout social media, frightening readers—including me. I don't live in the Pacific Northwest. And I have yet to visit Oregon, Washington, or British Columbia. But I have plenty of friends and acquaintances who are pastors and writers who live there. Not to mention readers! I ooh and ahh when folks post photos or videos of the area. How beautiful it is, and how I long to experience the beauty and culture and creativity myself—minus the dreariness and rain.

A few weeks prior to reading Schulz's article, I found out about an opening at a university in the Pacific Northwest. Not for me, but for my husband, Shawn, a philosophy professor. Although I was fairly certain he would get tenure at his current place of employment, one could never be too sure in academia, and so we had to keep an eye out for possible alternatives and opportunities. I told Shawn about the position and mentioned that he might apply "to see what happens." But then I read Schulz's article and firmly decided against it. "You can't apply! That school is in the area that will be destroyed! What if you are driving home and a bridge collapses on you or on the girls as you head to and from school? Or what if we are at the beach and a tsunami comes?" Imagining it and then saying it aloud twisted my insides. "Nope, we are not applying. We'll stick to the Midwest. I can handle tornadoes if we have a basement or shelter. I know what to do." I was familiar with tornadoes and terrified by earthquakes. Shawn didn't apply for the job.

A few years prior to that, I read an article about the supervolcano overdue for an eruption in Yellowstone National Park. "Great!" I told Shawn and others. "I've always wanted to go, but the minute I step foot in the park, it'll erupt and blow me to kingdom come." Shawn, trying to allay my apocalyptic fears (don't worry; I have my share of allaying his fears, which are different from mine), quipped, "Well, if it blows, then most of us in North America and probably here in Ohio won't survive since the ash will be in the air and possibly keep the sun from shining." His words didn't comfort me. As of today, I have yet to visit Yellowstone.

As an Enneagram Nine, a basic fear of ours is loss, or being disconnected. In this case it manifests as fear of losing my family and my life and everything that makes up my life. Being disconnected from Shawn and the girls would leave me fragmented and disconnected from everything I know. Everything familiar. Everything I love.

Interestingly enough, I sit here writing at our dear friends' home in Southern California. I flew out of Chicago to get here. Prior to my head hitting the pillow on the first night after I arrived, I foolishly googled "California earthquake zones." Guess where they live? Smack dab in the center of the San Andreas Fault! I was scared to fall asleep. *What if the earth begins to shake while I am asleep? What would I do? I'd be separated from Shawn and the girls. How could my friends live here like this?* Eventually, I thought to myself, *Bracing myself for an earthquake will do nothing to keep it from coming. I guess if I am going to die, I'll die here with Debby and Carl, separated from family.* And so, believe it or not, being here, knowing that a massive earthquake could happen any moment and yet not being able to predict it or prepare for it with much notice or with my family—and yet having the blessing of enjoying the Southern California weather in March—is changing me so that I take more risks and expend energy in moving beyond my comfort zones.

My time and your time are in God's hands. If we let comfort and safety rule all of our decisions we won't experience what life has to offer.

How has the fear of loss, disconnection, and fragmentation kept you from truly living? What step might you take to overcome it?

HUMILITY, ASSERTION, OPINIONS

SOMETIMES ON SOCIAL MEDIA I feel like I am standing in the center of a circle amid a family fight watching those surrounding me gesticulating, preening, scheming, manipulating, shouting, launching verbal grenades, or calmly and honestly sharing what they believe to be the truth. I see others standing on the sidelines because they can't get a word in edgewise or because they fear being assaulted by those who are more aggressive. Others head for the hills, disavowing social media altogether because they don't find it worth their time. Why would they willingly subject themselves to assaults on their identity and sanity?

Of course, as a Nine, I can see multiple sides. I can affirm kernels of truth on this side or that even though I don't think it is the complete truth or the full story. No one person or group has the corner on truth although some are much closer than others. I say this knowing I do not see everything, nor that everything can be seen in this life or even after—otherwise we'd be God.

I do see the value of engaging in social media and also the need to forego it in order to maintain our sanity. I regularly fast from social media whether that be throughout the day, for days on end, or on holy days.

This seeing multiple sides of an issue is so Nine-ish isn't it? That is why we are at the top or crown of the Enneagram—we can see the great expanse and have a little bit of all the other numbers in us. But the temptation is for us to stand in the middle and see multiple sides while never choosing or offering our own opinions. We fear displeasing people if we arrive at an opinion or a conviction they deem controversial.

But what if we are right, on point? The fact is, no matter how hard we try and no matter how right we are, not everyone is going to like us. Our Enneagram Nine temptation is to shrink back like a wallflower so that we don't offend. But moving toward health means we will work to know what we think and share our stances more often than we are comfortable.

For Nines, speaking truthfully and confidently—even if our stances on run-of-the-mill and controversial issues offend others—is one of the healthiest things we can do. We don't have trouble with humility, so let's remind ourselves again: we have to assert ourselves.

In what area(s) do you need to speak truthfully and confidently?

What would it take for you to risk offending someone for the sake of integrity and righteousness and justice?

WHAT IS LOUDEST
IN YOU?

IT IS SO HARD SOMETIMES TO KNOW what we want as Enneagram Nines because of the ease with which we merge with others. Are we wanting what we want, what others want, or what we think others want for us? When we've merged with others for so long, we lose sight of our own identities, our own agency, and of what we want.

When counseling college students and other adults in the area of passion, vocation, and calling, or writers who are stuck and have no idea what to write about, I ask them, "What is loudest in you right now?" That is, what do you think about all the time? What do you think about and do in your leisure time? For example, I never, ever think about spreadsheets, numbers, or mathematics.

However, day and night I do think about the gospel and how to apply it to everyday life. How to be like Jesus. How to better form pastors and lay leaders in the way of Jesus and make disciples who are more like Jesus. I think about the gap between what I say I believe and how I live. And I pray to God to close that gap because I want to be like Christ. I know people are watching what I say and do. In conjunction with that, I think about those we have hurled to the lowest rung of society and how the church treats them. And why the church more often than not treats them with contempt even if we profess love and compassion. My call is to serve the church through my presence: my physical witness, my writing. I've accepted that I am a doctor of the soul, a doctor to a sick church. I am to do my part in the name of the Father, Son, and Holy Spirit to bring her back to wellness. Of course, all is done in the strength of the Holy Spirit and in community. These are the loudest things in me and what have determined my vocation and calling.

Are you struggling with figuring out what you are supposed to do now? What is loudest in you?

GETTING AWAY WITH IT

ONE OF OUR STRENGTHS AS NINES is the ability to present the hard to swallow with a spoonful of sugar. We really do have an uncanny ability to make the medicine of tough realities go down. Or at least we are often able to communicate truths in such a way that people can hear them. I generally have no idea what my husband, Shawn, is talking about when he says, "I don't know how on earth you got away with that one!"

For example, one time I confronted a man about his marital infidelity and a single woman about being his mistress. My younger brother happened to be with me at the time. I asked the man if his wife knew he called and went to see this particular woman. "After all," I said, "if your conscience is clear, and as you maintain, you're not doing anything wrong, then why not let your wife know where you are?" And then I said, "Would you be okay with your children knowing?" I asked the woman, "How would you feel if this were being done to you?" I finished with, "You know it's not right." Afterwards, my brother, marveling at what I said, told me, "There's no way I'd be able to do that, Marlena, although it definitely needed to be done." Listen, I certainly don't get my jollies out of such confrontations, in making people squirm. But the circumstances did call for me to confront the illicit couple.

Nines certainly do not tend to like confrontation, though they can confront people. I think I get a holy boldness, a strength to kindly and assertively confront, when I see injustices and obvious wrongdoing and innocent people being hurt—especially by those who claim to be Christian. I don't expect non-Christians to act like Jesus, although some certainly act more like him than certain professing Christians! How infuriating.

On those occasions when Shawn claims, "You got away with it," I was just being myself. I didn't memorize my words ahead of time or script my responses. I went with the conversational flow. Of course, it entailed reading others' verbal and nonverbal cues and responding to those. My aim wasn't to lampoon characters or make someone feel uncomfortable. Every time it was a call to goodness and flourishing. A call to stop hiding and to do what is right. I really did have their best in mind.

Nines are renowned as diplomats and peacemakers. Good diplomats and diplomatic people have to say hard things and engage in difficult negotiations. But perhaps they are able to do what they do because multiple parties see that a good diplomat has their interests in mind too. I do think most people know we Nines have their flourishing in mind, because we do! There are no hidden agendas. No manipulation. Our identities and egos are not intertwined with or dependent upon their doing what we want. With us, what you see is definitely what you get.

Can you remember a time when you had to communicate hard-to-swallow information? How might you leverage that skill in your life?

TO-DO LISTS

THERE WAS A TIME WHEN I DIDN'T carry my phone around with me. If people wanted to get in touch with me and I wasn't available to pick up my phone, which was a home landline, they'd leave me a message after hearing, "Hi, this is Shawn and Marlena's. We are not available to pick up the phone right now, but leave your name, number, and a message. Then we will return your call as soon as we can." That was the message on our answering machine in 2007.

Back then, our schedule seemed simpler too. But that was because there were only two of us in the household, so I didn't have to write a lot down. Our rhythms worked like clockwork. Church, school, youth group, homework—we were both in graduate programs, Shawn studying for his PhD and me in seminary obtaining my master of divinity. We could keep track of our own schedules and had youth group meetings and events regularly scheduled.

But now we have three girls, and text messages can interrupt my concentration or whatever I am doing. The twenty-four-hour news cycle that I can access on my phone can clog my mind. I am getting older too. I forget things. So I have to write things down. I have to make a to-do list to keep me focused and on track.

As I glance at my to-do list today, I have a variety of things written down. *Mail the prayer quilts and include a card. Prepare for the retreat* (which I am leading). *Turn in your reimbursement form to Sarah. Check on babysitting for Valentina. Move writing money received to savings. Pick up Valentina, Iliana, and Isabella*—Shawn has meetings and can't pick anyone up. And there's more: *Make sure Iliana has something to eat after track and before soccer. Go through mail. Get three devotionals written. Answer emails and check calendar to schedule talks. Remember you have to write that book report for the publisher. Start it. Fold laundry. Make cookies/bread for neighbors. Meet new neighbors.* A lot of these things have to be done today. Of course, not all of them, and I know I won't get to some for weeks. However, I am scared that with everything going on in my head, with all of my responsibilities, urgent and not, I could forget some really big thing to do today. Although I've never forgotten to pick up any of the girls from school, I wouldn't put it past me. I have to keep things at the forefront of my mind.

Under stress, we Enneagram Nines can get scattered. Even amid a cascade of good news and new and good opportunities, we have to keep track of life. Lists help us to lasso our scattered minds to turn our ships back in the right direction. This morning I wrote the above list in my planner. It has a space for "priorities." My priorities today are to write the devotionals, pick up the girls, and start that book report for the publisher. I'd like to fold the laundry, but honestly, there is a good chance I will put it off until tomorrow. I know, I know, it could be wrinkled. If that's the case, I'll stick it in the dryer for when someone has need of a particular article of clothing. I have other priorities, and it is not at the top of my list today. We'll see what happens. If I don't do it today, I'll bump it up in priority to tomorrow night.

Do you have a to-do list? What do you need to prioritize?

ASKING FOR HELP

RECENTLY I SAW FRIEND who is an Enneagram Nine tweet that he felt "like a bother." He mentioned not engaging people on social media or in real life because he didn't want to bother them. In a private message, I told him he wasn't a bother; he had much to offer. In fact, he is a gift! I wasn't flattering him. What I said was true. We Nines have to strike the *I feel like a bother* thoughts down, take them captive, and transform our minds by transforming our thoughts that we might move forward in health and wholeness to actively use our gifts for the world.

When I was in labor in the hospital with our first child, Iliana, I only called the nurse once. Fortunately, I had Shawn by my side the whole time to help me. I knew the nurses were busy, and I didn't want to bother them if Shawn and I could take care of whatever it was on our own. The only time I did press the red call button for a nurse was around three in the morning. No one came. I really needed her. I found out later that there was a dire emergency—a mother and child in distress. I too had an emergency, though not as dire. Thankfully, soon enough the doctor came to check on me, and it all worked out. My sister is a nurse and has told me about how some patients treat nurses. I didn't want to be *that* overbearing patient that my sister and so many other nurses have encountered. So I didn't ask for help until there was an emergency.

I've gotten much better than I used to be at asking for help. I push through the *I feel like a bother* mentality. And the thing is, I don't mind if people ask *me* for help. I really don't. Shawn and I both are available to people and will do what we can within our means and within healthy boundaries to help and to be present. It is a ministry of availability. We make space or rearrange our schedules for others. We find this important especially in our society where healthy and helpful family members are not always close by.

Unfortunately, even though the Christian community is supposed to be the very last place that we should feel like a bother, sometimes we are made to feel like it through spoken or unspoken communication within that community. But there are many Christian communities who are most welcoming and wonderful and who invite those seeking help and healthy relationships.

Jesus himself asked Peter, James, and John to be with him on the worst night of his life, the night before his crucifixion. He asked them to hold vigil with him, to stay awake as he prayed in anguish in the garden of Gethsemane (Mark 14:33). He needed their physical presence to help him through the night. He relied on their friendship.

So, Nines, if people offer to help us, let's take them up on those offers. And also, let us have the humility to ask for help when we need it. Let us also believe that we have much to offer and that people enjoy spending time with us because they do, especially when we are ourselves and don't hold back. One way we self-forget, which is tied to our vice of slothfulness, is by not voicing our needs or desires. We simply do not think our needs or desires are as important as those of others. That is false. God will surprise and bless us through the generosity and presence of others. Jesus was not averse to asking for help nor welcoming people into his presence. He also made his own needs known to his friends. You are not a bother!

Have you ever felt like a bother? How do you combat those feelings?

Practice telling people how you feel and asking for help or the presence of others. Phone a friend or someone you admire to talk through your feelings. After all, Jesus confided in others.

SEEING

WE'VE BEEN LIVING IN OUR HOUSE ONLY ONE YEAR. The elementary school Valentina, my middle daughter, attends is between Pine and Mulberry streets, one block away. Next school year, our little Isabella will begin kindergarten. Our location makes us "walkers." All three of our girls, including our oldest, Iliana, will be walkers next year. Her school is on the opposite end of our street. But this story is not about her because she departs for school earlier. The only time we drive our daughters to school is if it is bitterly cold outside or if Shawn has to drop Valentina off on the way to his job because one or both of us are unavailable to walk that morning.

We notice, or at least should notice, the world about us as we trod back and forth on a regular basis to the elementary school. For example, last fall we stumbled upon a black walnut on the sidewalk. It is bigger than a golf ball but smaller than a tennis ball. Our family has a habit of kicking black walnuts ahead of us like little soccer balls whenever we are on a family walk at local metro parks. When we find them along our path, which is plenty during the fall, we kick them back and forth to one another or launch them way ahead of us down the path. We love our little black walnut soccer games and are eagerly on the lookout for the right ones to use on our walks. As it grew colder, we decided to place the black walnut we found on our walk to school in a divot next to the yellow fire hydrant. It is now spring, and much to our delight, the black walnut is still there, though now brown instead of bright green. I told Valentina and little Isabella, who accompanies us though she is not yet in school, that we could take the black walnut out when the ground dries up and our path is not laden with puddles or snow.

I've noticed other things since we've lived here. After losing my job due to budget cuts, I've been home during the day. I've witnessed lots of people getting pulled over by the local police on our twenty-five-miles-per-hour street as I work on writing projects by the picture window near our front door. The elementary school at one end, the junior high on the other end, daycares, preschools, banks, medical offices, and stores in between, in addition to the residential area, make our road a main thoroughfare and also a speed trap. Police are out and about to keep the children safe and to line the city's coffers. At the picture window I see many regulars: walkers, joggers, and dog walkers. Just yesterday I saw what I assume to be a grandmother pushing a stroller with a preschooler in tow. Also, while writing at our picture window, I've had a chance to regularly encounter our mailman, Don. We each wave hello. I wonder about Don's life. Who is he in addition to his role as a mailman? Does he wonder the same about me? Like about why I am now home every day? There is a whole world of life in this one human being who I wave to most every weekday morning. Yes, we left him a gift card for the holidays. Still. I doubt we will move any further than waving hello, except for that time I engaged him in conversation to find out his name and if he had any preferences for gift cards.

I remember what it feels like to feel invisible. And although I rarely feel that way now, maybe empathy is part of the reason I seek to render visible the invisible and those rendered invisible by others—to see the mysteries in these moments. We Nines are good at that. It is, in a small way, seeing as God sees. And that is a gift.

Take a walk or drive around your local neighborhood and pay attention to what you notice. With that, consider: Do you allow yourself to be seen by trusted others?

How might God minister to you through seeing and allowing others to see you?

NINE WITH AN EIGHT WING

I AM FAIRLY CONFIDENT I AM a Nine with an Eight wing.

Here's why: according to Suzanne Stabile and Ian Morgan Cron in their book *The Road Back to You,* an Enneagram Nine with an Eight wing is "one of the most complex combinations on the Enneagram given the Eight's need to go against power and the Nine's need to avoid conflict. . . . Talk about a walking contradiction!" I do feel like a walking contradiction, and sometimes the tension they describe is great within me. When I see people being mistreated and oppressed by those in power, when I see or experience injustice, my first inclination is to say and do something—not stand idly by. But then I think about the repercussions of my words and actions—conflict, job and opportunity loss, shunning, challenging, and attacks on others and myself can feel like opening up Pandora's Box. And I have lost a job and opportunities because I spoke up against injustice. I blew the whistle—so these aren't imaginary fears. That is my Eight wing getting me in trouble for justice.

Even though I didn't choose to be this way, to find myself in the school of biblical prophets "It is what it is," as they say. What I say and do can and will be used against me when they are not welcomed. Like the prophet Jeremiah, I have fire in my bones as I seek to honor and follow Jesus. I am not trying to start something. But even Jesus, who was perfect, ticked people off by telling the truth and by living faithfully. So I can expect to be lampooned and excoriated by some of my hearers no matter how gentle I am. However, maybe people will build tombs, offer awards and accolades, or say, "She was right!" posthumously (Luke 11:47-51)—but I'm not holding my breath.

Do you see the complexity for a Nine with an Eight wing? We seek to be peacemakers and reconcilers. But telling the truth and living truthfully will mean we are disruptors and interrupters for the sake of the kingdom. Left to myself and my own comfort, maybe I'd go along to get along and play like an ostrich and stick my head in the sand. But I simply can't. That would make for atrocities, as history bears witness. So here I stand.

It can be complicated being me. Yet all in all, I wouldn't want to be anyone else.

> **Are you an Enneagram Nine with an Eight wing? Do you know any? How might you spot them?**

CONFLICTED IN PARENTING?

IN AN EMAIL CONVERSATION WITH Suzanne Stabile, she wrote, "Nines have the least energy of all the numbers because they try to keep in anything that's going to cause trouble and try to keep out anything that's going to steal their peace." But apparently Nines with an Eight wing have more energy coming from that Eight wing. Still, we battle low energy.

Just recently my oldest daughter, who at this point is thirteen years old, described me as, "Funny, kind, caring, smart, fun, generally peaceful and seldom getting angry or raising your voice." Sounds good doesn't it? But she also added "unenergetic" to the mix. When I asked her what she meant by that, she said, "When you write, you have no energy left for anything else like going shopping for clothes or going on a drive." I took slight offense and asked, "But don't we go on family walks and hang out in the yard talking or reading or other things?" "Yes," she admitted.

And yet her comment makes me feel conflicted. I am her mother, a good mother by her own testimony (as she has told me other times). And yet, I am "unenergetic" in certain areas like when it comes to shopping and going on drives (and presumably other areas).

Interestingly enough, some have said, "I don't know how you do as much as you do. I certainly couldn't do it." Well, the thing is, both observations are true. My daughter is right about not having energy after I write. And I have been writing a lot for the last two years. Outsiders to the family see me when I am writing and speaking. I have energy and am extremely active in those areas, including justice issues because that's where I choose to put my energy. However, it leaves less energy for parenting. And I feel bad about it. Conflicted.

As driven and engaged as I am, I realize I can't maintain those energy levels for everything. When people call me "superwoman," I always tell them, "You don't see the piles of laundry stacking up (or my daughter calling me 'unenergetic' for that matter). Also, there's no way I could do what I do and parent my three daughters well without Shawn's help. He picks up the slack." If I am writing and engaged in justice issues a lot, I have lower energy levels for the rest of life. If I am highly engaged in the rest of life, I have low energy levels for writing and being active in justice initiatives. Something or someone(s) suffer. I am no "superwoman." I just have help.

Getting back to Stabile's comment, when I am writing or taking action in an area of justice, I have to keep things out, shield myself, so I can write and act. I also have to have a relative state of peace internally.

Should I give up writing and engagement on justice issues and only focus on parenting? I'd be conflicted about that too. And I think I'd be completely miserable and a bad parent. Whatever I do, I have to seek the kingdom of God and his righteousness so I can prioritize the most important (see Matthew 6:25-33). All this reminds me again that not one of us can do everything. I can't keep lots of balls up in the air. I have to acknowledge that even though I am a Nine with an Eight wing, as my daughter pointed out, I still come off as "unenergetic" to my family when I have been pouring my energy into other things. "Come off" isn't even right. *I am less energetic.* So, I have to put boundaries, brackets, around my writing lest I continue to have low energy levels for my family and live conflicted.

Do you have low energy levels? Or more energy for some things than others? Are you conflicted about how to use your energy? Maybe it's not with kids but with something else.

SOCIAL NINE

I AM A SOCIAL NINE. I took a quiz given by the Enneagram Institute and found that my primary dominant instinct is social. What does that mean?

The Enneagram Institute describes the social instinct this way: "Most of us are aware that we have a social component, but we tend to see it as our desire to socialize, to attend parties, meetings, belong to groups, and so forth. The social instinct, however, is actually something much more fundamental. It is a powerful desire, found in all human beings, to be liked, approved of, and to feel safe with others." The social Nine is the most driven and engaged of the Nines—so they frequently mistype as Ones or Threes.

Finding this out was like having an alarm go off: "ding, ding, ding!" I am acutely aware of power structure and status in the world and my place in it—which historically has been on the lowest rung of society in America, given that I was born a poor Hispanic-Latina woman. It is easy to feel unseen and unheard amid the cacophony of voices and people jockeying for position—even in the church. It's not that I place myself in that position or status; it's just how it typically goes.

With my keen eye for status, I've observed that Jesus didn't seek status, fame, and renown. As he taught us, the way up in the kingdom is down. The greatest in the kingdom of God will be the servants of all. Jesus makes a beeline for the lowly, the poor, the marginalized in society, and the poor in spirit. As Jesus told us, "The greatest among you will be your servant. For those who exalt themselves will be humbled, and those who humble themselves will be exalted" (Matthew 23:11-12).

Being a social Nine explains in part while I'm highly relational—it adds oomph to my ability to love my neighbors in a pleasant way! It is why I go to bat for the underdog. It's a kind of comforting the afflicted and afflicting the comfortable.

I used to minimize myself by not believing that others were interested in what I had to say. Even though today I still see the pecking order, thanks be to God, I am not trying to fight or claw my way to the top. That doesn't mean I don't want to be known and loved, form bonds as part of a group, and be a team player. I most definitely do! I do want people to like me and approve of me—not, however, at the expense of me following Jesus and doing what is right. Being liked or famous is not my primary motivation. That shows growth, especially as an Enneagram Nine who is reluctant to rock the boat or cause conflict, doesn't it?

What role does seeking approval, fame, or power play in your life? Are there areas where you might need to move into a more active and social role to steward your gifts well?

NINE WITH A ONE WING

I AM PREDOMINANTLY AN Enneagram Nine with an Eight wing. I think my being a Nine with an Eight wing is why my friend Ashley Hales called me a "velvety firecracker." I will tell the truth directly and gently but with love—at least, most people testify it's gentle and with love, though inside of me it might feel like Fourth of July fireworks are going off.

However, One is also one of my wings. Thus, I certainly manifest aspects of a Nine with a One wing. Just as Enneagram Nines with a One wing manifest some aspects of an Eight wing. A main difference is that Enneagram Nines with a One wing are more refined while a Nine with an Eight wing is a little more rugged.

Nines with a One wing lean toward perfectionism, a defining characteristic of an Enneagram One. They work hard and are creative and also friendly. They can see what needs to be done and done right, more systematically and in a more organized fashion than Enneagram Nines with an Eight wing.

My mother-in-law is an Enneagram Nine with a One wing. One reason I admire her, in addition to her wild generosity of spirit, is because of her organizational abilities and precision. Every single thing in her house is in its place. Moreover, she is very systematic and orderly about how she does everything in her entire life.

For example, my husband, Shawn, can walk into her house and find anything. He says everything is in the same place it was in 1986. That does not happen in my house! I mean I try to have things in a general order, in a general area, but she is so precise and organized it blows me away. She finds pleasure in organizing spaces. For me it's a chore. Though I am just as fastidious about some things like writing and editing my work!

My mother-in-law is an anchor and steady influence on us all. I've told her a thousand times, "You should work as a professional organizer." People pay a pretty penny for what she does so easily. I often ask her for ideas for how we should arrange our storage. Hard as I try, I can never be quite like her—and yet we are both Nines!

Are you a Nine with a One wing? Or do you know one? What do you observe? What gifts do Nines with a One wing bring to the world?

COMFORT, COMFORT!

I LOVE BEING OUT IN NATURE, experiencing the beauty and taking in the wonder of God's creation, but I am not interested in roughing it through rugged camping experiences. I want my shower and a comfortable bed and to smell good. I suppose it's part of the reason I don't sleep on airplanes or in cars. I don't sleep well anywhere except my own bed. Honestly, I hadn't thought of this before learning about the Enneagram. But it all goes very well with my Enneagram Nine desire for peace within and without. Physical comfort.

It is why I am not interested in any of those physical fitness experiences meant to show how physically beastly and rugged a person is. It might be an experience where a person trains for months to endure forty-eight hours where they pick up logs, walk or run through bogs, go on forty-mile walks—all the while prodded and yelled at by a former Navy Seal. When they finish the experience, their muscles seize up and they can barely walk. Our friend Chris is one of those tough-as-nails guys engaging in these experiences that also require mental endurance. I think

Shawn could easily do this too, if it was a priority. But me? I have no interest.

I do think about comfort and having the basics of money, housing, and physical health. Maybe growing up poor explains the reality that when I worry, I tend to worry about having enough money. It's also why I cling to Matthew 6:25-33, especially verse 33: "But *seek first* his *kingdom* and his righteousness, and all these things will be given to you as well" (emphasis mine). "All these things" are what we need. Of course, God's idea of what we need and our idea of what we need could be different. I think it's also why I love being at home and arranging my home environment in such a way that it is a peaceful refuge. It's not quite a spa; we have three girls. But it is the peace I can manage.

Funny thing is that the gospel calls us to give up our lives, our comforts, and our efforts of self-preservation to follow Jesus. Am I willing to do this? I think so. The season of Lent, the discipline of prayer and fasting, and the discipline of engaging in life—something that can be hard for Nines who would rather withdraw—push us in the direction of nailing our self-preservation to the cross to follow Jesus.

Where does comfort and self-preservation manifest itself in your life?

What are healthy and unhealthy aspects of it that you see?

DON'T PUSH ME!

LET'S TALK ABOUT COMFORT, ROUTINE, and how to anger a Nine. I hate to admit it because, hey, who likes to put themselves in a bad light? But I've discovered the truth is that as a Nine, I don't do well if I am being pushed. What do I mean by being pushed? Someone relentlessly breathing down my neck and badgering me. That leads to anger and withdrawal in me. (See, I am self-aware!)

As I write, we are in the midst of the Covid-19 pandemic. The five of us are at home and cooped up. We try to get outside as often as possible because we all love being outside. And yet we've had a run of rainy, thirty- to forty-degree days. So we are homeschooling: instructing, watching, and teaching. Our girls aren't just reading assignments and doing homework. We are all engaging each other. And all the while, Shawn and I are trying to work.

Having constant noise, breaking up fights, and having to be "on" continually is difficult for my disposition and Shawn's too. I lean toward the introverted side, and he is definitely an introvert—an Enneagram Five. Oh, of course we love our girls. We spend lots of time with them even when there is no pandemic. We enjoy them and the creative and interesting personalities that God gave them. Our relationship with them is of utmost importance. The difference now is that there is no downtime. We seek to protect their health, our health, and the public's health by our isolation at home. I am sure they'd like downtime from us too. In fact, I know they want to go play and hang out with friends!

Part of the reason this pandemic has revealed irritation in me is because, as with everyone else, my routine has been upended. During the day, I have in mind what I want to do and what I want the girls to do. I have my plan for what I would like to do and accomplish each day—but inevitably, the plan is interrupted. The isolation and quarantining during this pandemic have revealed just how irritating it is for me to have *my* schedule and routine thrown off. I am pretty accommodating most of the time—after all, I am a Nine, aren't I? However, with no margin and little time for myself and constant interruptions of my work, in addition to monthly hormonal fluctuations, I am fit to be tied. Newsflash! I can be hard to be around sometimes too, despite how agreeable I am in general.

If we are learning anything as Enneagram Nines, it is that we, too, have weaknesses and have to stop seeing ourselves with rose-colored glasses. We are neglectful. We can be irritating to others though our penchant is to run away from admitting it! I can readily see why Enneagram experts say we find comfort in routine. Constant interruption of our routine is akin to disturbing our peace. I can see now that they are right indeed when they tell us that pushing or pressuring us drives us to dig in. Sustained outward pressure on us is also disturbing to our peace. We like to get the job done, and we do get the job done without people, close family members or not, breathing down our necks.

It is good to know these things about myself. It is good to know from whence stem my reactions. And yet I cannot be content with mere self-awareness. I have to take the next step toward healing and transformation. Colossians 3:13 will help me along the way: "Bear with each other and forgive one another if any of you has a grievance against someone. Forgive as the Lord forgave you." I pray those closest to me will be able to do the same for me.

Do you get irritated when your schedule is interrupted? When pushed? If you are doubtful about that as a Nine, is it possible you are repressing those feelings?

SOMETHING YOU'VE NEVER DONE

BECAUSE WE CAN GET STUCK in our comfortable routines as Nines, we can inadvertently miss out on all the goodness life has to offer. And there is goodness, but sometimes Nines are asleep to it. As I said earlier, I grew up poor. There are a lot of opportunities and things I did not have while growing up—especially hobbies.

Often, we lacked food, money for gas, and the opportunities privilege grants. I couldn't afford to take music lessons. In sixth grade, I remember my mom telling me I couldn't take music lessons or be in band because we couldn't afford to rent the instrument. We didn't have gas for the trips to practices and games that were needed for me to be on sports teams either. I was in little league baseball and in softball in eighth grade because I got rides most of the time. I think it is the small things that many Americans take for granted that I didn't have—like music and sports and other hobbies.

And there were other ordinary joys I missed out on too. Little things, like flowers and bird feeders. I suppose it might've been poverty but not just that. It was the weight of additional sadnesses, the blanket of depression, and possibly personal preferences in my family that kept me from experiencing the delight of flowers and bird feeders.

In my adult life, I've awakened to how little birds and flowers are so dear to me. I am no longer asleep to ordinary little joys. I think much of it is due to how lovely they are and how Jesus tells us to consider the birds and the wildflowers when we think about God's care for us (Matthew 6:25-33). So last fall, I decided by faith to plant tulip bulbs and other perennials. At this point it's early spring, and I'm starting to see seeds planted in faith spring up. A wise soul, someone who knows about planting and such, told me to sprinkle cayenne pepper on the soil so the colony of squirrels that live on our property and adjacent properties would not dig up the seeds and bulbs we planted. I did as instructed. These flowers that were once seeds are my babies. Even now I pray, while my daughters are within earshot, that they wouldn't be killed by cold weather, snow, or a deluge. I pray that they would grow up. What beauty! What delight!

After visiting our friends Debby and Carl in Southern California and witnessing the variety of birds about their feeders, I decided that one of the first things I'd do when I got home is march over to the store and purchase bird feeders and shepherd hooks to hang them on. We put them up several days ago. That too was done in faith. I talked to Debby on the phone and lamented the fact that no birds have shown up. She assured me they would come. "The hummingbirds are still in the south and have to make their way north," she told me. "It is still cold where you live; the birds will come as it gets warmer." I sit here typing, looking out the window, believing that soon enough I will see the birds come to feast at the feeders.

One other thing I did is begin to learn how to crochet. My sister, who can pretty much teach herself anything by watching a video, showed me how to do single stitches. So, I've begun crocheting when I can snatch a moment. My goal is to make scarves and blankets, maybe hats, once I get the hang of it.

This last year, I resolved that I would try new things, be they little or big. I am making good on that resolution to wake to things I was once asleep to and am enriched because of it. How about you? Are you willing to exert the energy to try something new and delightful?

Think of one thing you can do that is new and different from the past. Bring joy into your life with the little things. Maybe pick up a new hobby? Being awake feels so good.

TRY SOMETHING HARD

DO WE DECIDE NOT TO DO SOMETHING because it is hard? Or because we are worried that we are too old, not good enough, not skilled enough, or _____. You fill in the blank. For a decade now I've been wanting to go back to school. *Wanting* may be too weak of a word. Part of my calling is to help form leaders in the church. For me that means either pursuing a PhD or getting a doctor of ministry degree.

In 2011, I told Shawn I had been thinking about going back to school for about a year. Our daughter Iliana was four. Not long after that conversation, I became pregnant with our second daughter, Valentina. After Valentina was born in 2012, I thought about going to school again. But I was still recovering from the pregnancy, delivery, and lack of sleep. In addition, a hostile takeover occurred where we worked, so we had to find new jobs—we couldn't stay where we were. There was no use in applying for a PhD program because I had no idea where Shawn and I and the girls would end up.

Thankfully, Shawn got a tenure-track position in philosophy right away. It's a good thing I didn't apply to school because we ended up moving away from where I was thinking about applying. Shortly after we moved, I became pregnant with our youngest, Isabella. She was born in 2014. Incidentally, she was born just a few months after my first book, *A Beautiful Disaster: Finding Hope in the Midst of Brokenness*, came out. There was no way I could go to school and work with three young daughters. I had very little time or energy or health to do much with my first book. I had about given up the ghost as far as school was concerned. But a year after I had little Isabella, I was offered a position as an adjunct professor at a local seminary, where I've been teaching since 2015. Already I was working part-time as the minister of pastoral care at our church, and Shawn was working full-time. We juggled childcare between the two of us.

Fast-forward. In 2018, I applied for a doctor of ministry program and was placed on the waiting list. I was planning on entering the next year, but then we had a series of unforeseen financial setbacks. I couldn't pay to go to school. I didn't understand why my road seemed to be blocked. I knew I was called to go to school. It would equip me to better teach seminarians and others. Well, I figured I should apply to a PhD program just in case I could get a full ride. But I almost didn't apply because to do so required me to take the GRE; I hadn't been in math classes since I was seventeen years old because in college I tested out of math. The only thing between me and applying to PhD programs was that GRE. I resolved I was going to take the exam no matter what. I set the latest date I could for the test so I had plenty of time to study.

Yes, I decided that even though I am an Enneagram Nine, I would resolutely engage and use all my energy to do the hard thing. I went to work studying. After work and after taking care of the girls, I studied late at night. Taking the GRE was the very hardest thing for me. It was my boogeyman. I feared taking it, but I did it. And I also applied to PhD programs. And surprise of all surprises, I got into one with all tuition expenses paid and with scholarships—a full ride! Had I let taking the GRE prevent me from moving forward I would never have had the opportunity to apply for a graduate program and receive a full ride.

What hard thing do you fear doing?

How is your fear keeping you from moving forward? Offer your fear to God and ask for a vision for moving forward.

BEING PASSIVE-AGGRESSIVE?

I HAVE READ IN SEVERAL PLACES that Enneagram Nines can be passive-aggressive. I don't think of myself as passive-aggressive. I know a few passive-aggressive people, and I am nothing like them. And yet I hear the phrase thrown around a lot. No one has ever accused me of being passive-aggressive, but it doesn't mean I don't have it in me, even though I try to be pretty direct. I have been told a few times that I am blunt. Still, I had to chuckle when I read this on the Integrative Enneagram Solutions website: "Many Enneagram Nines are unaware of their own passive aggressive behaviour patterns and how these affect others around them."

The Very Well Mind website calls passive-aggressive behavior "sulking, backhanded compliments, procrastination, withdrawal, and refusal to communicate." For example, procrastination is passive-aggressive when a request is made of a person and they procrastinate just to stick it to the person making the request. While I am not that kind of passive-aggressive, some Nines are. I am not the sort of Nine to give a backhanded compliment either, but some are. Although if Shawn and I get into a fight, I can withdraw. That is passive-aggressive.

And yet another passive-aggressive trait is to say, "I am not angry," when I clearly am. I'm guilty of this. But I didn't know I was being passive-aggressive in the moment—what I was trying to do was avoid conflict.

Another behavior I didn't know was passive-aggressive is avoiding people when we are angry. Guilty again! The reason I avoid people when I'm angry is because I don't want to unleash my anger upon them. When it has subsided, then I return. My anger doesn't last for long—usually. But that can be a form of passive-aggressiveness. Others might interpret this avoidance as giving them the cold shoulder. But in my mind, I'm only trying to avoid acting out in anger. What would be better and healthy is to be direct about the fact that I am angry—before I'm ready to blow my top. I have gotten better at this, but I still have work to do.

Another example of passive-aggressiveness is blaming others instead of taking responsibility for one's own actions. We see that often in marriages. Those of us around children have heard it from them—blaming the other instead of taking responsibility for their own actions.

We see passive-aggressiveness present in churches and workplaces. A person will deny being upset but then grouse to others about the pastor or situation. Some sabotage their own coworkers through passive-aggressive means: blame, procrastination, sulking, and backhanded compliments.

We Nines have to work really hard to admit our anger even though we don't like feeling angry. And from what I've learned, we have to be extra careful not to engage in passive-aggressive behavior. When we do, we should be ready to admit our contribution to the illness and destruction in the world and in our relationships.

Are you guilty of passive-aggressive behavior? Name the ways in which you are passive-aggressive. You might have to do some research on it.

COMPARING OURSELVES
TO OTHERS

DO YOU EVER CONSIDER OTHERS more beautiful, intelligent, clever, strong, or savvy than you? Do you believe you are always getting the short end of the stick?

Our tendency as Nines is to downplay ourselves and our abilities. We might find ourselves thinking that everybody but us has something to offer. I remember one of the first things Shawn said to me after we began dating—we were both twenty years old at the time—was that it is unwise to compare ourselves to others and that no good comes from it. *How astute. What wisdom comes from this young gun! It's probably a result of his experience,* I remember thinking to myself. His words made an impression upon me. Indeed, they fell upon me like a ton of bricks. We Nines twirl our heads and crane our necks this way and that, looking about at everyone else and seldom seeing ourselves. That has to change—for our health's sake, it must!

I'm going to ask you to take a moment to think about yourself. Set aside a few minutes to think about what *you* are good at. It might be extremely difficult because you may not think that you are much good at anything. I'd advise doing this after you finish reading these words lest you move on and forget. I also suggest taking the step of asking your friends what they think you're good at. You might ask them in person, send an email, maybe make a phone call, or venture onto social media. List out five to ten things you are good at. It could be concrete, like drawing, organization, baking, gardening, playing an instrument, or getting the best bargain at the store. Maybe you are good at fixing cars or computers. You get the idea. Or it could be things less tangible, like kindness, compassion, or being on time. Whatever it is, big or little, write it down. Take note of what others tell you too. Put it somewhere that you can find it and where you can refer to it often.

Sometimes, actually frequently, we need to look into the delighted eyes of others in order to see how our good God and beloved others see us. Hearing others name the goodness in us and about us, to us, is also one way God shows up in our lives. Obviously, don't ask those who find great joy in doling out criticism or who are studied in giving backhanded compliments or who are jealous of you. Ask safe people—those who want to see you and others flourish.

And then, do the same for others without them asking. Name the goodness in others. How beautiful is that?

In John 21, after Jesus prepared a post-resurrection breakfast for some of his disciples, Peter and Jesus went for a walk along the beach. In conversation, Jesus reinstated Peter after Peter had betrayed Jesus on the eve of Jesus' crucifixion. Then Jesus revealed to Peter the nature of Peter's death. Without skipping a beat, Peter looked back and noticed the apostle John trailing them. And then he turned to ask Jesus, "Lord, what about him?" (v. 21). Apparently not quite satisfied with what he heard about his own life, Peter quickly whipped his head around to inquire about what would happen to John. You see how quickly he moved to comparison?

Jesus' response to Peter reveals that Jesus would have none of it: "If I want him to remain alive until I return, what is that to you? You must follow me" (v. 22). Jesus' answer to Peter is the same to us. What's another person's life and trajectory to us? We must follow Jesus using our own gifts and abilities.

What are some of your gifts and abilities?

How can you affirm others in their gifts?

THEOLOGY OF PLACE

MY FAMILY AND I OFTEN WALK or drive to the Maumee River. It's a mile or less from our house, which is downtown.

River Road is where the big, expensive houses are. We can't access the river among the houses. But there is a small public park in our town along River Road. It honors Commodore Perry and local soldiers who died during World War I. A year or two ago, I noticed that most of the soldiers never saw war; they died of the flu.

If you walk or take your car down to the water, you'll be making a steep decline. When you make it there, the little area of public riverfront is right next to a boat launch. A picnic table is available, clumsily sitting on a small patch of grass. It's not the most scenic or accessible part of the river, but it will do. My family and I often just come to glimpse the river.

My daughters throw sticks into the water and then the whole family heave-hos its way back up the steep incline. Our choice is either to walk on the road or sidewalk or take steps at what appears to be a seventy-five degree angle.

Taking the steps allows us to see the monument of Commodore Perry and plaques honoring the soldiers who died of the flu. If we drive (or walk, if we want to go on a many mile walk), we cross the bridge between our town and the next. The river separates the two towns.

Crossing the bridge takes us to Side Cut Park, near where Shawn's dad is buried. Side Cut Park runs along the river. There we see deer, woodpeckers, goldfinch, blue herons (our favorite), turtles in a bog or on a log in the bog, and Canadian geese. We see people fishing. There are walkers and runners and the occasional cyclist. Farther away there are other parks along the Maumee, and sometimes we travel to them to be near our beloved Maumee River.

We go to see and seek some part of the Maumee and nature almost weekly. The contours and the ebbs and flow of the river are a part of our lives. It is shaping us, our outlook, our being. We depend on the Maumee River—in a different way than the Miami Indians to be sure. They lived here before us, driven off this beautiful land by settlers. I often think about the Miami Indians and their lives and how they depended on the land and on this river that starts in Fort Wayne, Indiana, and flows northward to empty out into Lake Erie.

I've talked about exercising and getting into my body and concentrating on one thing, the quotidian of the everyday, like laundry. Nines are supposed to be the most anchored to our bodies but easily disassociate from our bodies. I would like to draw us Nines back to ourselves and to our surroundings. Are you and I aware of our physical surroundings? Of the landscape and topography around us and of our neighbors? I wonder, how does where we live affect our theology, our internal landscape, our appreciation for God and neighbor? I have friends who live by mountains, some by the sea, others in arid places. Some live by forests and streams—landlocked. Others live among seas of golden wheat with very few trees. I live in the green spaces, with the four seasons, all of which form me.

How are you faithful and devoted to people and the place around you?

In an untethered world, how does the climate and topography—your surroundings—affect you?

GAINING ENERGY AND EXPENDING ENERGY

EACH ONE OF US HAS A LIMITED AMOUNT OF ENERGY. Our level of physical fitness and our stress levels affect how much energy we have. What we eat affects our energy levels. How we choose to spend our time does too.

Lately, I have been thinking a lot about what saps my personal energy levels. This is a partial list of what I have come up with: social media, poor eating habits, lack of exercise, failing to go outside into God's creation, lack of sleep, lack of in-person interaction, refereeing fights among my daughters and managing their moods, a messy and disorganized house, stress, and monthly hormonal shifts. I could list a lot more.

The more I learn about the Enneagram, the more I realize that as Nines our desire to be peacemakers and make sure everyone else around us is okay, including ourselves, also depletes us of energy. The thing is, we can't really escape being who we are. We can only seek to be the healthiest Nine we can be. And seeking to be a healthy Nine makes a difference even if it requires a little bit of energy! To be healthy, to love God and others well, to love our neighbors as ourselves, we will have to expend energy to have energy.

For example, the more we exercise, the more energy we will have for our daily activities of living. The same holds true for putting forth effort to keep our homes and environments organized. In my life, that not only requires organizing myself, but it requires continually nudging my daughters to organize themselves. And that is exhausting. But expending energy in the short term in the areas of my life I mentioned will have positive long-term effects. There are some things that I can control and much that I can't. There's little I can do to control the monthly hormonal shifts. I have to deal with those as they come. But, if I have attended to these other things under my control, it makes life easier and I have more energy.

The more I think about it, cramming my day with phone calls and virtual meetings is energy draining. I like to make sure what needs to get done gets done and that I fulfill my commitments. There is nothing wrong with fulfilling commitments. Yet, as I mentioned before on Day Twenty-Eight, it leaves less physical and mental energy to be present to my family when I stack my commitments up one upon another. When working from home it is best to space these things out and set boundaries and limits—like no work after 6:00 p.m. I also have to limit the amount of leisure calls I take in one day and spread them out too.

My goal for this week is to organize parts of my home. My room needs reorganized: I need to get rid of clothes I don't wear and books I don't read. I also need to organize and pay my bills. Next week I will focus on my exercise schedule. Thinking about what needs to be done for us Nines to have higher energy levels can be overwhelming. It is best to focus on one or two things at a time and then move on from there.

What saps your energy, keeping you from loving God and neighbor?

What do you have to put energy into in order to get more lasting energy?

What limits and boundaries do you need?

LEAD AND ENJOY

WHAT TYPE OF LEADERS ARE WE? Some Enneagram Nines won't take leadership positions because they require too much energy and because too much conflict is involved. Remember, we are habituated toward avoiding conflict and toward comfort. If we make ease and lack of conflict litmus tests for whether or not we'll lead or take on leadership positions, then we never will.

This is the type of leader I have been in my life: I speak wisdom into the ears of the kings or queens—that is, to the bosses or head honchos—and they listen to me. God has put me in positions to advise those who have the final say on decisions that affect lots of people. I suppose that is playing the role of an advisor and being part of an advisory cabinet. As a good Enneagram Nine, I don't feel the need to be in charge but will take charge if needed and if I witness incompetence. I am not scared to step up.

Don't let anyone tell you that as a Nine you don't make a good leader. Nines can be phenomenal leaders as they step into wholeness. That said, any leader who leads out of ego or ill health will not be a good leader no matter their Enneagram number. Nines have the ability to lead well. They can draw on their One wing, the reforming side and that which is concerned with living morally, to lead with integrity. They can draw on their Eight wing to follow through with energetic right action. That is what is so great about Nines: we will lead with right action and put ourselves and our bodies on the line to do what is right. We are activists with integrity. Not manipulating, not running over others, but inspiring others to right actions by the witness of our own lives and behavior. The healthier we are, the less we minimize or simplify complex problems and systems.

As Nines, we have a little bit of all the types at work in us. We can function as a charismatic and leaderlike Three when we need to do so. And we can think through decisions. However, if there is something we don't know or can't do, we have no qualms about admitting it. We simply ask or delegate it to the person most qualified in order to get the job done.

Plus, we Nines relate well to others. People trust us because we have proven ourselves trustworthy. We are willing to listen without inserting our agendas. Others know we have their flourishing in mind because we do. Those in positions beneath ours know we'll do our best to do right by them even if it means sacrifice on our part. Moreover, the further we move into health as an Enneagram Nine, with advice from the wise and expert around us, the better we are at making hard decisions, even if our decisions mean certain conflict and backlash or criticism against us. We can make decisions that are best and the least harmful to the most people. We do not elevate profits over people. We are true team players.

Maybe like me you have functioned mostly as an advisor. I've taken the lead role several times in my life, especially when it comes to justice, human rights, and cover-ups at Christian institutions. Note that I didn't say I *never* take on primary leadership roles, only that I most often function as an advisor. And if advising is your God-given role and gift, so be it. Make the most of it.

What leadership qualities do you see in yourself? Make a list of how you are using or not using your leadership abilities.

What, if any, primary leadership roles is God calling you to take?

FLOURISHING NINES

WELL, WE HAVE SPENT FORTY DAYS TOGETHER. We've reflected on much though not all the good, the bad, and the ugly of being an Enneagram Nine. When I first found out I was a Nine, my reaction was, "Oh no, not that one!" That reaction is often indicative of the Enneagram number we are. It's typical to be appalled by the weak areas of our Enneagram number and how they show up in our lives. So if you have been appalled by Nine weaknesses, you are in good company.

We need to remind ourselves that if we are going to be whole as Enneagram Nines, we have to tell the truth about ourselves to ourselves. That was our first matter of business on day one. It is of utmost importance to tell the bad and ugly truth, to confess our unhealthy dispositions and sins to God, ourselves, and trusted others that we may be healed (James 5:16 and 1 John 1:9). It is also healthy and whole to own up to our gifts and abilities. We should shout them from the rooftops to ourselves and rejoice!

We are indeed good at many things. Our lives are peaceful refuges for people. And for goodness sake, people like us and enjoy being around us. We are not off-putting. As we move into our health and strengths we gain confidence and become self-possessed. We don't shrink from or shirk life or responsibility. We can make smashing leaders without the ego that brings so many down. We are cool, calm, and collected, especially in the midst of upheaval and in a polarized world. We can see the good, if there be any good, on many different sides. And the further we move along in health, the more quickly and confidently we stake our claims with opinions we might have been too scared to share in the past. We take a stance even if it might upset others around us. At the same time, we major on the majors and minor on the minors. We will not be leading a church split because we don't like the color of the carpet or the new building even though we have opinions about them both. It's because we can see the big picture.

As we move toward wholeness, we become aware of our feelings, especially anger, instead of disassociating from them. We admit to ourselves and to others that we are angry and irritated. We become more aware of our bodies. Instead of mindlessly eating and neglecting ourselves because we are too busy merging with everyone else, we pull back to know and take care of ourselves.

What is extremely beautiful, and what I find refreshing and a great gift, is that our holy idea is holy love. And our virtue is right action. No wonder I have always loved the apostle John, the apostle of love, and the Gospel and epistles he wrote. First John 3:18 captures it: "Dear children, let us not love with words or speech but with actions and in truth." For me, everything—every thought, word, and deed, even what is buried deepest in the caverns of my heart— must spring from love of God and lead to love of neighbor. I am not content to talk about God and the ways of God to people; I want to live like Jesus in the life he has given me! And if it is not done in love, I am just an annoying noise, a clanging, shrill cymbal (1 Corinthians 13:1). It's useless.

My desire for us Nines is that we would flourish—that we would be the best we can be with what God has given us. Let us mourn and lament our sins and weaknesses, but let us celebrate too! There is much that we contribute to the world. Let us never forget it!

What qualities of a Nine do you rejoice about?

After these forty days, what one or two qualities will you move forward to develop?

ENNEAGRAM
DAILY REFLECTIONS

SUZANNE STABILE,
SERIES EDITOR